SEX OFFENDERS:

Approaches To Understanding And Management

Adele Mayer

L$_P$ **LEARNING PUBLICATIONS, INC.**
Holmes Beach, Florida

ISBN 0-918452-95-3

Learning Publications, Inc.
5351 Gulf Drive
P.O. Box 1338
Holmes Beach, FL 34218-1338

Printing: 7 6 5 4 3   Year: 7 6 5 4 3

Printed in the United States of America.

Table of Contents

Preface

105164

PREFACE

For four years, I facilitated a large, constantly growing and evolving outpatient therapy group for sex offenders referred by the court system, adult probation, adult parole and other city agencies. For two years prior to the onset of the offenders therapy group, I had specialized in working with survivors of intra- and extra-familial molestation of all ages. Then, as a female therapist and a humanist, I had believed that it was more logical and ethical for me to work with the victims, rather than the perpetrators of sexual abuse. Working with adult victims, however, often necessitated involvement with their spouses, some of whom were sexual offenders and/or victims of abuse themselves. Also, due to a dearth of available local outpatient services, I received a number of requests to work directly with perpetrators. As the Program Director of one of the largest sexual assault centers in the country, I had the opportunity to assess, provide, and oversee therapeutic services for literally hundreds of victims, spouses, and offenders. During that time, my perspective broadened as my insights deepened.

One of my areas of work relates to child victims and the many issues involved in dealing with a population that is basically powerless, and on the deepest level, easily manipulated. These children are a population victimized largely by adult males and then literally forced to defend themselves within a male-dominated system. On many occasions, I testified in superior, juvenile and domestic relations courts, sometimes as an expert witness and other times as a therapist for child victims or adult rape victims as well as for sexual offenders.

Because of my work with male offenders, I was often in the "privileged" position of being perceived by the court as relatively unbiased and not simply as a female victim-advocate. In other words, it was not easy for defense attorneys to impeach, discredit, and dismiss my testimony as a therapist, albeit female, because I devoted considerable time and effort to treat the very population whom they were defending for crimes against women and children.

In the past several years, I have often wondered if the tax-paying public is aware that field workers in sexual abuse sometimes

v

feel as powerless as the victims. My peers and I refer to the legal process as a "game" in which the rules constantly change with an unpredictability that shocks and astounds participants, a game which the players with the most money, sophistication and power inevitably win. Women and children rarely have the most money, sophistication and power.

To indict the criminal justice system alone, however, is misleading. The therapeutic community bears some responsibility, too, for the misuse of power bestowed upon it by a nation that places trust in the inherent honesty of professionals. Unfortunately, these professionals sometimes know and understand less than the public at large and their interests center around self-aggrandizement. Many politicians, too, in an effort to attain status and recognition, while enhancing their popularity among the voting public, espouse causes simply to meet personal goals with little or no consideration for either the ethics involved or the long range implications of their positions.

While I have no final answers for these concerns which effect all of us on some level, I believe that the information contained herein regarding therapeutic interventions and assessment with sex offenders is valuable for therapists and others involved in case management and planning. I hope that the lasting benefits of this book will be in helping all concerned to view the issues involved in victimization from a broad-based orientation.

My approach to understanding and assessing sex offenders is based on the need for workable controls rather than untested claims regarding cures. It is similar, in some respects, to the approach employed by Alcoholics Anonymous and other self-help group models, and derives some of its principles from Henry Giarretto's group treatment model for incest offenders and their families, Parents United and Daughters and Sons United (PU, DSU).

Started ten years ago, PU and DSU are self-help components of the Child Sexual Abuse Treatment Program, itself a part of a co-ordinated approach to the management and treatment of incestuous families, linking Child Protective Services, adult probation and county attorneys.

I advocate an interdisciplinary approach to both theory and therapy that encompasses psycho-sociological, biological, historical and economic factors. Reducing sex offenders to oral-dependent, compulsive personalities with unresolved infantile longings, is probably as absurd as viewing all deviants as products of emotionally and culturally deprived social and economic backgrounds where the value system promotes exploitation of women and powerless children.

The book poses a number of questions and offers some tentative answers. This questioning is valuable since one aspect of our societal character relates to an apparent need for definitiveness, closure and immediate resolution of conflict, often at the expense of truth and honesty. Willi, a German-Swiss psychiatrist, highlights the difference between the European and American approach to problems.* The European seeks to understand the problem; the American, to immediately solve it. Perhaps our young and impatient culture can learn from Europeans whose tradition has taught them that the complexities of human nature cannot easily be comprehended nor reduced to simplistic explanations and solutions.

One final cautionary note must be stressed. Successful treatment of a very select, carefully-screened, group of incest offenders may be possible, although as yet we have few, if any, methodologically-sound, longitudinal studies to demonstrate either treatability or effective treatment modalities for this population. We have even less information about the etiology, diagnoses, prognoses and effective treatment measures for other sex offenders such as rapists, fixated pedophiles, exhibitionists, voyeurs and others. Overzealous therapists, sometimes motivated by needs for status and financial gains, must be very careful not to make unfounded pronouncements concerning the efficacy of treatment methods being used with sex offenders and regarding any positive prognoses for these sexually aggressive men.

---

*Willi, J. COUPLES IN COLLUSION: The Unconscious Dimension in Partner Relationships. Claremont, California: Hunter House, Inc. 1982, Preface to the U.S. Edition.

In light of our current state of relative ignorance regarding most aspects of sexual deviance, both ethically and legally, therapists should be held accountable for erroneous claims made to the courts and probation/parole regarding treatment of a population that threatens the emotional, psychological and physical safety of society.

PART I:

UNDERSTANDING AND ASSESSING SEX OFFENDERS

1

TYPES OF SEXUAL OFFENDERS

Deviations, abnormalities, variations, aberrations and perversions in human sexual behavior are endless in number and kind. Likewise, theories regarding the classification and causation of these behaviors are numerous and often contradictory. The result: confusion which is further compounded by the current rise in the social acceptance of aberrant behavior when such behavior, often and arbitrarily, is classified as victimless.

Therefore, an examination of the issues related to deviant sexuality reveals inadequacies regarding both theory and treatment. Lester (1975) reports that common etiologies are ascribed to all deviations and that theories do not distinguish among the various deviations. Stoller (1975) notes that there is a dearth of material on aberrant sexuality and that the literature rarely reports on syndromes other than homosexuality and fetishism.

Since 1980, there has been an increase in the literature on sexual deviations. However, the body of the new literature does not compensate for the lack of solid material prior to this decade and it does not provide us with much-needed longitudinal studies.

In case management and treatment, professionals must cope with these inadequacies related to theory and treatment. Additional problems are posed by the legal system where psychological disorders result in criminal behaviors punishable through incarceration. In addition, professionals have traditionally focused on symptoms and syndromes in our classification of deviance. For example, an exhibitionist may be recognized as manifesting voyeuristic behaviors, but the only emphasis in his classification will be on his being an exhibitionist.

Despite current knowledge of the phenomenon of progressive deterioration (the gradual escalation of sex offenses over a period of time) exhibitionism is isolated as a treatable problem in itself, without considering the possibility of future deviance, such as fetishism or rape.

Thus, there are numerous difficulties inherent in presenting an overview of deviant sexual behavior. Specifically, there are complications involved in defining, describing, and classifying sexual aberrations. Lester (1975), author of a review of the literature on sexual deviations, reports that there have been inadequate studies and research on fetishism, pedophilia, incest, rape, exhibitionism and voyeurism, as well as on obscene telephone callers.

Approaches to Deviance

A number of approaches to the study of deviant behavior evolve from psychological and sociological theory. Likewise, much confusion (in terms of definitions, categorizations and etiology) exists among theorists, even as they attempt to arrive at an understanding of deviant behavior.

One approach, which is oversimplified, yet relevant to treatment, focuses on the various models of deviant behavior from which social and legal sanctions, i.e., religious, legal, medical and labeling models are derived. The religious model relates causation to demonic possession; the legal, to criminal behavior; the medical (including the analytical), to illness; and the labeling, to categories of behavior. From these models, professionals have derived widely divergent treatment approaches, including exorcism, social control, and incarceration.

For clarity and conciseness, this section briefly describes the commonly-accepted deviant behaviors, their definitions and their manifestations, without focusing on fine distinctions in classification, labeling and etiology, and without considering moral or legal arguments regarding the normality or abnormality of variations in sexual behavior. Deviations are seen as fantasies that are acted upon and that arise from threats to sexual identity (Stoller, 1975).

To further facilitate an understanding of aberrant behavior, deviations may be understood in relation to a number of variables, such as the type of sexual object (pedophilia), the mode of gratification (voyeurism), the intensity of the gratification drive/frequency (satyriasis and nymphomania), and the context of arousal (group sex).[1]

In general, men exhibit deviant sexual symptomology to a much greater degree than women. Money and Tucker (1975) report that men are more vulnerable to all kinds of psychosexual nonconformities. The term paraphilia refers to conditions involving bizarre imagery/actions necessary for sexual excitation. For example, many of the paraphilias including voyeurism, exhibitionism, necrophilia,

---

[1]Groth, A.N., and Burgess, A.W. "Rape: A Sexual Deviation," Paper presented at the American Psychological Association Annual Meeting, September 5, 1976, Washington, DC. Groth and Burgess concisely described the generally accepted definition of deviance, which they, in turn, reject in favor of a conceptualization based on the psychological dynamics underlying the sexual behaviors.

and lingerie fetishism appear to be limited to males. Hence, the deviations presented in this chapter are ascribed to males, with an understanding that females, too, can be incest offenders, pedophiles, and exhibitionists.

Rape

Rape is commonly defined as forced sexual contact without consent. Statutory rape is sexual contact by a person over the statutory age with an individual whose age is less than some stipulated age. As with other sexual deviations, Lester notes, research studies on rape have been inadequate.

A number of studies on rape rely on projective testing which lacks both reliability and validity. Nonetheless, Groth and Birnbaum (1979) describe the biological, psychological and social aspects of rape, as well as the characteristics of rapists, based on several studies of offenders. The rapist lacks victim empathy, objectifies others and has few intimate relationships.

Stress often precipitates deviant acting-out behaviors. The rapist is seen by some to be an angry and/or inadequate individual with low impulse control and general criminal tendencies (Lester, 1975).

Unlike incest and pedophilia, rape has been associated with the lower socio-economic classes (Smithyman, 1979). Recent studies indicate otherwise. Some show that large numbers of men, in general, condone rape and/or would attempt rape, if assured of immunity. More specifically, one study, involving a random population, focused on undetected rape among members of white collar and upper socio-economic classes.

A major limitation for accurate data-gathering stems from reporting problems. The FBI reports that a rape occurs every few minutes in the United States (1984), and yet, few rapes are reported. Only a few of the many rapists are apprehended and even fewer of those apprehended are convicted. Also, when convicted, and if incarcerated, rapists generally serve only two to three years in prison.

Groth and Burgess (1976) have classified rape according to underlying motivations. According to their classification categories, power rape, which comprises over fifty percent of all reported sexual assaults, involves the need to control and overpower the victim and often is premeditated.

Anger rape, usually unpremeditated and constituting under fifty percent of reported cases, has the additional components of contempt and hostility. In anger rape, the desire is to inflict harm and express revenge and retaliation. Sex is used to humiliate, abuse and degrade. Sadistic rape, comprising less than one percent of reported cases, may involve mutilation, ritual and murder.

Groth and Burgess (1976) characterize rape as the sexual expression of nonsexual needs, and the rapist as having unresolved feelings that might be related to unconscious incestuous desires, and to heterosexual or homosexual anxieties. Rapists under study admitted being unable to ejaculate at the time of the assaults and did not rape for sexual gratification but, rather, to fulfill other needs related to conscious or unconscious anger, control and power. These authors describe the phenomenon of "progressive deterioration," i.e., the gradual escalation of sex offenses over time. More than fifty percent of their sample of offenders had prior convictions for rape; over one-half of the recidivists (more than twenty-five percent of the sample) showed an increase in their use of force over time; a number of the offenders admitted to having committed prior undetected assaults; and many of the men had been juvenile sex offenders.

In recent years, incidences of rape of the elderly, often by adolescent males, have increased, as have the categories of gang and marital rape. In his study, Blanchard (1959) highlights what some believe to be the homosexual factors in gang rape, such as the sharing of female sex objects and eroticized adulation among group members.

One of the more interesting, albeit controversial, studies of rape involved the wives of rapists (Palm and Abrahamsen, 1954). The wives were found by objective observers to be masochistic, passive and submissive in their marriages. They presumably negated their femininity, were perceived as sexually unresponsive by their spouses, and were believed to have covertly encouraged aggression in their husbands.

Another recent study by psychologists Michael Petrovich and Donald Templer (Psychology Today, October 1984, 80) indicates that convicted rapists report a high rate of heterosexual molestation as children, i.e. molestation by females. In their sample of eighty-three convicted rapists, they report that, before the age of sixteen, fifty-nine percent had been heterosexually molested by older females. The authors conclude that some rapists may want to punish their victims as a result of their own early abuse. However, Petrovich and Templer are clear to note that the high correlation between molestation and rape does not necessarily imply causation.

The studies cited provide interesting data for professionals. However, before any definitive conclusions are formed regarding rapists, more longitudinal, methodologically sound, empirical research must be conducted.

Pedophilia (Pederasty[2], Pederosis)

The term pedophilia (child love) includes a wide array of sexual offenses, but always refers to molestation of a minor child by a pedophile (child lover). There are heterosexual, bisexual, and homo-sexual pedophiles—some of whom incestuously abuse their own children. Pedophiles derive psychological, emotional and sexual gratification from children.

---

[2]*Pederasty* is anal coitus with a male minor; *pederosis* is the use of children as sexual objects.

Their compulsive sexual orientation begins in the teen years or younger, and their offenses include emotional seduction, photographing and/or prostituting of children, single or multiple incidences of child rape, as well as long and short-term molestation of a few or as many several hundred children in a lifetime. Pedophilic activities often are premeditated and are not necessarily precipitated by causal stresses. The preferred child victims, with whom the offenders identify emotionally and psychosexually, generally fall into definite age ranges, i.e., one pedophile may prefer children from age six to ten, while another may choose children from age nine to eleven. However, victims can be of all ages and of either sex.

Pedophilia is linked to child pornography and prostitution, and there are a number of underground networks promoting the legitimacy of adult sex with children (Mayer, 1985). Among the various organizations promoting the spread of pedophilia is the Rene Guyon Society whose credo is, "Sex before eight or else it's too late," and NAMBLA (North American Man-Boy Lovers Association). Both groups boast of having thousands of members.

Statistics on the prevalence of pedophilia are difficult to compile, although the incidences of sexual offenses against children are staggering. Most cases of extrafamilial molestation are not reported. In a study of 100 pedophiles, Roxxman (1976) reports that less than one percent had been arrested. Of those arrested, less than three percent had been incarcerated.

In the existing data we do have, incest offenders often are grouped with pedophiles. However, professionals who treat sex offenders, separate those incest offenders who molest exclusively within the home, from pedophiles whose primary sexual orientation is directed toward children in general. Differing dynamics between the incest offender and the pedophile necessitate separate treatment approaches.

Pedophiles tend to be immature, lonely, socially isolated, inept, shy and passive men who relate to children more comfortably than to adults, and who genuinely appear to care for their victims. They fall into all age groups, and they may be married, divorced, separated or single. Pedophilia also cuts across socio-economic classes.

Until recently, there has been very little information regarding the etiology of pedophilia (Lester, 1975). However, in 1979, a study indicated that perhaps as many as eighty percent of pedophiles had been sexually abused as children. Therefore, the underlying dynamics of pedophilia appear related to early, unresolved trauma, such as identification with the aggressor, repetition compulsion or displaced anger. In conclusion, the authors categorized pedophiles either as fixated or regressed. Fixated pedophiles are emotionally and psychologically "stuck" at an early age (often the age when their trauma occurred) whereas, under stress, regressed pedophiles revert to early modes of (fantasized) gratification (Groth and Birnbaum, 1979).

As with other sexual offenders, pedophiles manifest antisocial behavior, including low impulse control, an absence of guilt and remorse, objectification of others, transitory and shallow relationships, and irresponsible behavior. They characteristically deny or minimize their offenses, in part to justify deviant behavior, and sometimes project blame onto their victims. Hence, they are an extremely difficult population to treat, and the prognoses usually are poor (Mayer, 1985).

Incest

Incest, or intrafamilial molestation, is sexual contact among family members not related by marriage. Incest is widespread in the United States and is believed to affect at least one in ten families (Geiser, 1979). In recent years, there has been an alarming rise of reported cases nationwide. Incestuous behavior includes a wide spectrum of activities including verbal and physical exhibitionism, fondling, digital or penile penetration of the vagina, sodomy and rape. Molestation may occur once, infrequently or frequently over a period of years.

The most common form of incestuous behavior is father-daughter or father-stepdaughter incest, although grandfathers and uncles also number among the perpetrators. In any case, men comprise the majority of the offenders and female children constitute most of the victims of incestuous abuse. Brother-sister incest probably outnumbers father-daughter cases, but is considered less damaging to victims, especially if the siblings involved are of a similar age. The damage, however, can be quite severe if there is a wide discrepancy between the ages of the perpetrator and the victim.

Incestuous behavior tends to be inter- and intragenerational, occurring within and between generations, and is strongly affected by situational factors. Dysfunctional relationships, chemical abuse, sexual problems, social isolation and other stresses all contribute to the onset of incest in families. In addition, certain personality types are at high risk for molesting their children. Character-disordered men with low impulse control, low frustration tolerance, thwarted dependency needs, low self-esteem and the need for immediate gratification appear to be at high risk. Like pedophiles, many incest offenders had been sexually and/or physically abused as children (Mayer, 1985). Unlike pedophiles, incest offenders' primary sexual orientation is toward adult women. However, they use their victims as substitutes for mature sexual partners.

Family dynamics must be considered when describing incestuous behavior. The literature variously describes incestuous families as enmeshed, collusive and accommodating. Wives are seen as "silent partners" who unconsciously or covertly encourage molestation. The incestuous triad, composed of offender, spouse and victim, is seen as functioning pathologically with distorted roles where the child victim often assumes the wife's position in the family by meeting the offender's sexual and emotional needs.

Generally, incest in the family begins with fondling when the oldest female child reaches five or six years of age. Victims do not disclose sexual abuse because they fear being disbelieved, blamed or held responsible for potential family disruption. Hence, in the absence of outside intervention, the behavior continues and progresses until it culminates in intercourse by the time the child reaches puberty. Sometimes disclosure occurs early in adolescence when the victim fears pregnancy or reacts to paternal prohibitions regarding her desire to expand her social horizons. Typically, offenders deny their offenses, at least initially. However, many of the men eventually confess to molestation in order to spare their child victims the ordeal of the court process.

Despite the burgeoning number of treatment programs for incest offenders and their families, very little is known about   incest, its etiology and its relationship to other sexual offenses. Like pedophiles, a number of incest offenders were sexually and/or physically abused as children, and the underlying dynamic, such as displaced anger or identification with the aggressor, may be functioning.

A deeper understanding of incest offenders, may reveal that they share many of the characteristics of other sexual offenders and that too heavy a focus in their therapy has been placed on the understanding of family dynamics. In recent years, for example, research has shown that incestuous offenses often begin when the victims are toddlers or younger and that the children frequently are physically hurt or seriously frightened by the victimization. Furthermore, incest offenders have histories of undetected sexual offenses besides incest, and some of the offenders are, in fact, pedophiles with a decided sexual preference for children. However, at this point, clearly more research is needed before practitioners can implement new treatment programs, except on an experimental basis.

Exhibitionism (Indecent Exposure, Adamism[3])

Exhibitionism is defined as repeated exposure of the genitals or the entire nude body to an adult or child stranger to achieve sexual arousal. Masturbation may or may not accompany exposure. Exhibitionism is largely limited to male offenders and, when the

---

[3]*Adamism* is defined as nude exhibitionism.

victims are children, the deviant behavior is seen as a prelude to more serious pedophilic acts (American Psychiatric Assn., 1980). The age of onset for exhibitionist behavior is usually at puberty with peak incidences occurring between fifteen and thirty (Lester, 1975).

Rickels (1955) discusses three kinds of genital exhibitionism, i.e., ego dystonic (or compulsive), where there is an absence of impulse control; depraved, where there is impotence, emotional immaturity and exposure of the genitals to children; and organically impaired, where there is carelessness, social obliviousness and often, the inability to distinguish between right and wrong. Other authorities variously describe exhibitionists as narcissistic, passive and sadistic.

As with other sexual offenses, psychological studies regarding the etiology of exhibitionism have been inadequate (Lester, 1975). In general, it is believed that the act of exposure is intended to cause fear in women who are perceived by the exhibitionist to be powerful and castrating. Thus, exhibitionism is seen as an act of contempt with a need to humiliate. Often, there are sado-masochistic elements involved in indecent exposure. The roots of this deviation may relate to an early childhood traumatic experience where sex was associated with shame and disgust, and where there was a resultant infantile fixation (Veraa, 1976).

Langevin (1983) outlines the various theories regarding exhibitionism. Factors associated with this deviation include marital problems, fear of females, sadism, hypersexuality, nonassertiveness, pedophilic tendencies, unconscious homosexuality, auto-eroticism, and courtship disorder. With regard to courtship, behaviors follow four phases, i.e., searching for a partner, pre-tactile contact, tactile contact, and genital intercourse. Voyeurs are believed to be blocked at phase one; exhibitionists, at phase two; and rapists, at phase four (Freund, 1982).

Exhibitionists are described as anxious, timid, passive men with poor self-images. They are insecure, socially shy, eager to please, and often fairly responsible.   Generally, these men are of average intelligence, from all socio-economic classes, and either married or single.   Several authorities note that voyeurism often accompanies exhibitionism.   Psychosexually immature, exhibitionists are described as suffering from castration anxiety and the need for reassurance of their masculinity.   They tend to be ambivalent toward women and often are perceived as mother-wife dominated (Veraa, 1976).

One aspect of exhibitionism that appears to have been neglected in the literature relates to the concept of progressive deterioration. Exhibitionism often has been viewed as an isolated symptom. However, even within the limits of what is known about sex offenders, their histories reveal progression in the increase and severity of offenses from adolescence to adulthood.   For example, the criminal histories of a number of rapists indicate that their sexual offenses began in adolescence with exhibitionism and voyeurism.   Hence, professionals should be aware of undetected offenses in the histories of the offenders whom they treat.

Finally, some theorists posit that a number of exhibitionists want to be apprehended and that, unlike the voyeur, the exhibitionist is self-punishing, careless, and cavalier in his behavior in order to "be stopped." Few clinical studies corroborate this assumption. There may be other motivating factors to consider, and professionals must be careful when formulating post-facto assumptions to explain seemingly irrational behaviors.

Voyeurism (Scoptophilia, Peeping Tomism)

Voyeurism is the act of looking (peeping) at people who are naked, disrobing, or engaging in sexual activities to derive sexual excitement, and is often accompanied by masturbation. This deviation appears to be chronic, limited to males, and usually begins in early adulthood.   Often, it is associated with exhibitionism.   In addition, many rapists have histories involving both exhibitionism and voyeurism.

Lester (1975) reports that voyeurs are a heterogeneous group in terms of their social class and ethnic backgrounds. Many of the men have inadequate sexual lives and are quite passive. Nonetheless, voyeurs can be potentially dangerous, especially if acting-out behaviors are a prelude to more violent crimes such as rape. Several authorities report that there appears to be a sadistic component in voyeurism, i.e., in degrading women and seeing them as vulnerable and helpless. The deviation has been likened to visual rape.

The genesis of voyeurism may lie in childhood trauma, with some contending that its origin is in viewing sexual intercourse with a resultant castration anxiety, or in the acting out of parentally thwarted desires to witness nudity or intercourse (Langevin, 1983). The voyeur unconsciously attempts to relieve anxiety by re-enacting the primal scene (sexual intercourse) and may feel reassured through further identification with the father-aggressor. Yalom (1960) hypothesizes that voyeurs have an infantile wish to view female genitals, to see that the lost or fantasized penis of the woman actually does exist. In addition to castration anxiety and exhibitionist tendencies, voyeurs may have homosexual tendencies related to early trauma and stunted heterosexuality (Lester, 1975).

However, most of these theories regarding the etiology of voyeurism are hypothetical, based on anecdotal data. Hypotheses based on poor sampling techniques can, unfortunately, be quite dangerous. Too often, treatment plans, prognoses, and recommendations are based on poorly formulated theories and unsystematically-gathered data.

Interestingly, there may be a relationship between pornography, striptease shows, group sex and voyeurism. Many authorities agree that a connection exists but the conclusion is still tenuous, possibly because voyeurism involves illicit and socially unacceptable behavior and is difficult to isolate and measure.

Fetishism

The Diagnostic and Statistical Manual of Mental Disorders (DSM-III), 3rd edition, describes fetishism as the use of nonliving objects as the repeatedly preferred (or exclusive) means to excite sexual feeling (American Psychiatric Assn., 1980). Fetishism is the symbolic use of nonsexual objects or body parts for sexual arousal. A chronic disorder, rare in females, fetishism is distinguished from behavior involving the use of sexual objects (such as vibrators, specifically designed for sexual stimulation) as well as from transvestism in which female clothing used in cross-dressing is not meant to sexually arouse the user. The fetish object may be used alone or may be integrated into sexual behavior with a partner.

Stoller (1975) broadens the definition of fetishism to include necrophilia and behavior in which human beings are treated as organs or as role players, such as victims, slaves or beaters. Other authorities, however, believe that broadening the definition of fetishism bars methodologically-sound research based on homogeneous populations. Socarides (1960) notes the most common fetishes as shoes, feet, corsets, and underwear. In fact, there has been little definite research on fetishists (Lester, 1975).

Fetishism is first noticed in adolescence, although it is believed that the object of choice actually begins to assume significance earlier in childhood. Psychoanalytic theory seeks to attribute causation to castration anxiety, while learning theory proposes a conditioning etiology. Schmideberg (1972) believes fetishism is a factor in exhibitionism. Fetishists, some believe, defend against castration anxiety with the hostile and symbolic element of taking and hoarding what is forbidden.

A Few Conclusions

In reviewing each of the major sexual deviations, described or mentioned, it is clear that more research and data-based hypotheses are needed. At the present time, the literature presents a mixture of theories of which many are psychoanalytically-based and generally lacking in credibility. These theories are reworked and rehashed, and offer little justification for serving as a foundation upon which to base treatment modalities.

Among the few generalizations that can be formed from the current body of knowledge are the following: 1) men commit a variety of sexual offenses about which little is known; 2) anger, related to unresolved childhood trauma, appears to be one common denominator in many of these offenses; and, 3) offending behavior can, and often does, become compulsive and subject to progressive deterioration.

It is interesting to speculate on why so little is known about sexual deviance which undoubtedly has existed since the beginning of history. One wonders if denial or minimization, rooted in male prerogative, is operating within our culture. If the state of our knowledge has been affected by cultural defenses, the situation is unfortunate, not only for the victims but also for the sexual offenders. Given societal norms, it is clear that deviants suffer consequences from their uncontrolled impulses—not just legal consequences, but intrapsychic stresses and societal pressures as well.

2

ANGER:
A Key Factor in Sexual Offenses

Incest perpetrators and other sex offenders often have histories of having been sexually and/or physically abused (NBC, 1984). In one study, seventy-five percent of the 150 men were sexually abused as children (Foster, 1981). The literature also indicates that a great number of these adult sexual offenders experienced childhood conflicts and traumas which have 'resulted in anger that often has been suppressed, repressed, or otherwise redirected. However, while the role of anger has been examined in violent sex offenses, it has not been examined adequately in the so-called nonviolent sexual offenders with the possible exception of the exhibitionist who is perceived as hostile to women and seeking reassurance of his masculinity (Brecher, 1979; Groth, 1979; Cohen, et. al., 1975). Nevertheless, the backgrounds of both violent and nonviolent sex offenders often are markedly similar, in that their histories are characterized by having experienced both physical and sexual abuse.

Repressed anger, anger denied on a conscious level to avoid accompanying fear, guilt or anxiety can lead to the eventual overt expression of impotent rage, psychosomatic illness, suicidal ideation or attempts, passive-aggressive manifestations, displacement or projection. The precise source of the anger may never be known or discerned. What is clear, however, is that anger is energy and, like any other form of energy, it eventually seeks release, sometimes in convoluted, indirect and disproportionate ways.

In addition to abusive backgrounds, a number of incestuous perpetrators appear to have experienced what Gregory Bateson refers to as "double-bind parenting," i.e., parenting involving conflicting and often directly opposing messages regarding the appropriateness of certain behaviors and the acceptance of certain emotions. An example of "double-bind parenting" involves a mother who simultaneously shows physical affection toward her child while verbally berating him for some infraction. Double-bind messages simply compound and magnify the problems inherent in experiencing and expressing anger appropriately.

The backgrounds of other incest offenders reveal an authoritarian style of parenting, common in abusive homes, where emotions are closely monitored and suppressed and where verbal and nonverbal parental admonitions control behaviors. Authoritarianism contributes to repressed/suppressed aggression (Bach and Goldberg, 1975).

Alice Miller, a practicing psychoanalyst in Zurich, paints a powerful picture of angry and violent behavior resulting from authoritarian, abusive and neglectful styles of child-rearing (Miller, 1983).

Madow (1972) refers to the fusion of aggression and sexuality in all sexual acts and to the presence of hostile components, even in simple expressions of affection. Kinsey (1953) notes that there is a physiological similarity between sexual arousal and anger. For those sex offenders whose backgrounds have been fraught with conflicting messages, deprivation, sometimes violent parenting behaviors, and possible physical and/or sexual abuse, this fusion of sex drives with aggressive or violent ones is often distorted or exaggerated, finding release in deviant sexual behavior marked with clearly observable hostile or aggressive components. Bach and Goldberg (1975) note that the two major sources of repression, and the primary source of emotional and interpersonal problems in society, are repressed sexuality and repressed anger.

Accordingly, anger appears to play a role in the commission of sex offenses. Recognizing the roots of this anger and its various manifestations may help to facilitate an understanding of both the etiology and the dynamics of sexual abuse, which, in turn, may contribute to the formulation of more precise treatment strategies.

Prescott proposes a multi-causal theory of violent behavior including biological, environmental and social factors. The author also notes that early deprivation influences the brain's chemistry and structure, resulting in aggressive adults.

Anger is a complicated emotion with many manifestations and derivatives. On one end of the continuum are mild irritation, annoyance, impatience, and resentment—feelings within an individual's control that enable him or her to maintain a sense of equilibrium. On the other end of the continuum are explosive rage and uncontrolled violence—feelings that manifest themselves in perverted and antisocial behaviors. When suppressed, anger mounts to the boiling point, and, in the process, corrodes and distorts other feelings.

Anger is an emotion that can give its possessor the illusion of having power and control. However, it often masks fear, hurt, depression, guilt and frustration. For the sex offender with feelings of inadequacy and conflicts which center around dependency-autonomy, anger can be a comfortable emotion, providing temporary relief from the more painful feelings of vulnerability, fear and rejection which lower self-esteem. The projection of responsibility, displacement of feelings and provocation of conflicts may help the sex offender experience anger and avoid close self-examination.

Manifestations of Anger

There are a number of overt patterns of behavior which result from anger. Each one may have its own unique history and consequences.

Passive-Aggressiveness

The passive-aggressive personality fears anger and retreats from direct encounters, using the primary defenses of denial, projection and displacement.   For example, after a mild disagreement with one's spouse, in which rage has been suppressed and marked by slightly hostile barbs, a person might "accidentally" spill coffee on his or her spouse's favorite garment.

The passive-aggressive personality avoids intimacy and close interpersonal relationships.   He or she objectifies others while impersonal, material gains become of paramount importance in providing satisfaction.   This personality type is manifested as withdrawn, detached and passive.   Ironically, such a coping style leads to a self-fulfilling prophecy.   Passivity and noninvolvement often elicit punishment and rejection from others, which further reinforces withdrawal and detachment.

The covert or hidden anger of the passive-aggressive personality typifies many incestuous offenders.   Like the child who fears parental wrath or disapproval, the incest offender often fears rejection, condemnation or, perhaps, his own potential explosiveness.   Thus, direct manifestations of healthy and appropriately-expressed anger are avoided at all costs.

An example of incestuous abuse as a result of passive-aggressiveness can be found in one thirty-eight-year-old perpetrator who fondled his stepdaughter for two years and finally confessed during a marital therapy session.   This man eventually learned in therapy that he sexually abused his stepdaughter to "get back at" his wife who rejected him sexually, belittled his career endeavors, and had engaged in frequent extra-marital affairs.   Another offender, also covertly angry at his ex-wife for her domineering behavior during their marriage, subsequently molested his natural teenage daughter during her weekend visits.   After six months of group therapy, he was able to recognize that his feelings of impotence and rage against his wife were displaced from her to his daughter who "looks just like my wife."

Both of these offenders, incidentally, had been sexually abused as children. The roots of their original anger appear to relate to feelings of powerlessness during childhood abuse. Anger was triggered unconsciously and displaced during subsequent life trauma that elicited similar feelings of helplessness.

Regression

Child molesters often have been characterized either as regressed or fixated. For regressed offenders, cross-generational sexual activity is activated by stress; for fixated offenders, attraction to children is compulsive and stems from arrested sociosexual maturation (Groth, et. al., 1982).

Many of the characteristics of incest offenders are similar to those of young children. These men often have primitive or under-developed moral consciences, poor impulse control and low frustration tolerance. They engage in expedient and self-serving behaviors and do not experience empathy for others. Like the toddler whose needs and wants are thwarted, the incestuous adult often is demanding, volatile and explosive.

In group therapy sessions involving incest offenders and their spouses, an informal count was taken regarding the incidence of battering. All twelve of the wives present at the session stated that on at least one occasion, they had been struck by their spouses. Also, many of the men had physically abused their male offspring during the same period of time that they were sexually abusing their daughters/stepdaughters. Displays of violent aggression often relate to the low frustration tolerance, low impulse control, and poor problem solving skills that are characteristic of immature and self-centered individuals.

Unlike the rapist who is often seen as motivated by overt power needs, eroticized rage or sadism, the incestuous offender is usually perceived as less violent and dangerous. Groth describes three basic patterns of rape: anger rape, in which sex becomes a hostile act; power rape, in which sex is an expression of conquest; and sadistic rape, in which anger and power are eroticized.

The role of anger in the commission of incestuous abuse, however, may well have been minimized in the literature in an attempt to differentiate among the characteristics of the various types of sexual offenders. However, anger seems to be present as a motivator for incest offenders, although possibly to a lesser degree than in rapist. The point is that caution is needed in regard to the elimination of anger as a factor in incest.

Hospital personnel, police investigators and social workers in the field easily can attest to the fact they are seeing growing numbers of incest offenders who have raped and sadistically tortured their victims. In fact, a number of victims present evidence of physical trauma and even larger numbers of victims contend that they have been threatened, even with death, by the offending parent who uses any and every coercive measure to prevent disclosure.

Rogers and Thomas (1984) report that among child molesters, a common method of coercion is physical force followed by physical threats. Parental offenders use threat of harm (forty-five percent) or physical force (forty-four percent) as often as other kinds of offenders.

When one considers the fact that one-third of all cases of sexual abuse have occurred by the victim's ninth year of age, one realizes that molestation by an offending parent is emotionally, psychologically and often physically traumatic for young child victims (Borowski, 1985). Many child victims recount episodes of pain during digital penetration or attempted forced penile entry as well as feelings of suffocation during forced fellatio.

In just ten months of private practice, I personally received over fifty referrals of sexually abused children aged seven years and under. Over ninety percent of those referrals involved intra-familial molestation (incest). Many of the young children were emotionally traumatized and a number of them had been physically hurt by their fathers, stepfathers and or grandfathers during the molestations. Several cases involved mothers who had fled from other states, in violation of court orders, to protect their three-, four-, or five-year-old daughters and sons from further traumatization by the natural fathers.

In one case, a five-year old girl had been forced to defecate on her father following fellatio. In another, a three-year-old girl, complained that her father persistently refused to allow her to urinate and repeatedly "squirted white stuff" (ejaculate) on her face and hair. A four-year-old boy suffered rectal lax tone following repeated insertion of drum sticks by his natural father.

Because the child victims were five years of age and under, they were unable to testify in court or even to verbalize consistent disclosures regarding the details of their abuse. As a result, criminal charges were not filed, although police reports had been made. Without corroboration from the criminal courts, civil court judges refused to bar visitations by the offending male parent during divorce proceedings. Allegations of coaching by mothers were not involved in these particular cases, possibly because the disclosures occurred prior to, and prompted, divorce actions. Allegations of coaching regarding molestation now are commonplace in divorce-custody proceedings, although there are no data to indicate if the incidence of coaching has increased because of the publicity surrounding child sexual abuse.

Incest offenders often fear their own anger and the response that its manifestations might elicit. Hence, they tend to hold in feelings, to internalize guilt and blame and consequently end by experiencing depression and anxiety. Stored anger finds eventual expression in the passive-aggressive behavior described above or in an explosiveness when the offender is thwarted or frustrated. Of course, the net effect of storing anger and eventually exploding in pathological behavior is an exacerbation of the original fears and a further diminishing of self-concept.

Defensive Reactions

Conscious and unconscious defensive reactions are involved in all aspects of human behavior and certainly are present in passive-aggressiveness and regression. Special consideration, however, should be given to two psychological defenses, identification with the aggressor and displacement, because they are characteristic of a number of incestuous abusers who were sexually and/or physically abused in childhood.

The incest offender who has been psychologically, physically and/or sexually traumatized in childhood may identify with the offending perpetrator or aggressor as an unconscious protective maneuver. Later in life, when he becomes the victimizer, he re-enacts the trauma experienced as a child, but, this time, his role invests him with the power and control he lacked as a child victim.

Other adult offenders, also traumatized in childhood, unconsciously displace onto child victims, the original anger they harbored against their own perpetrators. In situations involving both identification with the aggressor and displacement, anger plays a key role in the victimization of children. Here, anger appears to result unconsciously. The original traumatizing event promoted anger, frustration and impotence, later expressed in distorted and convoluted patterns of behavior.

Treatment Implications

In working with sex offenders in general, and incest offenders in particular, therapists need to address the issue of anger directly by using a variety of treatment strategies.

For example, the therapist can facilitate insights by helping clients understand how passivity leads to unexpressed or stored anger. Clients might be helped to understand that the short-term rewards for suppression may lie in a temporarily conflict-free environment, but that the long-term effects can be disastrous. Clients need to know that violent, uncontrollable outbursts (triggered by perhaps insignificant events), psychogenic illnesses, and suicidal acts (or their equivalents) can result from stored anger.

When dysfunctional patterns are identified, the therapist needs to develop appropriate treatment strategies, including the following:

1) Affective, experiential work for releasing anger (bioenergetics, gestalt role plays and others). For example, a sex offender with a traumatic childhood history can be helped to relive the original trauma with accompanying anger against the offending parent and with resultant catharsis through pillow-pounding, by "facing the perpetrator" in role plays, or by direct confrontation with another adult victim who has a similar abuse history.

2) Assertiveness training practiced in therapy on a systematic basis and geared toward helping the offender clearly distinguish among passive, assertive and aggressive behaviors.[4]

3) Stress management, including the cognitive understandings of dysfunctional patterns of coping, and the role of stress in emotional, mental and psychogenic illness, as well as training in deep muscle and autogenic relaxation and work with visual imagery.

4) Didactic material on both sexuality and chemical abuse, showing their relationship to anger, including the exploration of covert and direct manifestations of aggression in sexually deviant behavior; also, the relationship between chemical abuse and lowered inhibitions.

---

[4]One of the best texts for any client population is Bower, S.A., and Bower, G.H. *Asserting Yourself: A Practical Guide for Positive Change.* Reading, MA: Addition-Wesley Publishing Co., 1976.

5) Behavioral management techniques for fostering the identification of events that trigger anger, along with the presentation of a breakdown of the components leading to aggressive release and the substitution of alternate, tension-reducing behaviors.[5]

6) Reality-based directive techniques, including environmental manipulation for sublimation, and the rechanneling of energy into constructive, socially-acceptable outlets.

Restated, anger is a key determinant in the commission of sexually deviant behavior. In order to provide case management, supervision, or therapeutic interventions for offenders, service providers must understand the etiology of anger, its complicated manifestations, and the various interventions that are specifically geared to help perpetrators manage stress and frustration in ways effective enough to curb deviant manifestations of anger.

---

[5]"The Social Readjustment Scale," *Journal of Psychosomatic Medicine,* 1967, 2, 213, developed by T.H. Holmes and R.J. Rake, is a useful assessment instrument to help clients evaluate stress levels. There are many excellent books about stress management the market. A good description of the overstressed, Type A personality can be found in: Friedman, M., and Roseman, R.H. *Type A Behavior and Your Heart.* New York: Fawcett Crest, 1974.

3

ASSESSMENT

Assessing sex offenders to determine potential or actual deviant behavior is a very difficult task because:

1) The etiology and nature of sex offenses have not been fully researched for data;

2) Sex offenders exhibit no set personality profile;

3) The threat of criminal prosecution precludes honest self-reporting;

4) Sex offenders tend to be manipulative and expedient, thus diminishing the likelihood of honest and accurate self-appraisal and self-disclosures;

5) Bias and conflicting values among evaluators exacerbates existing confusion; and,

6) No formal testing devices exist to measure the credibility and deviant acting-out behaviors of accused or admitted offenders.

Complexities of Diagnosis

The literature reflects the problems that result from the over-simplification of issues related to the causation, treatment and prognosis of sex offenders.   Incest offenders, for example, have variously been classified as authoritarian tyrants, regressed pedophiles, symbiotic introverts, alcohol-dependent personalities, and sociopaths.   The reality is that many factors—including cultural, psychological, genetic and environmental—contribute to the development of deviance.   In recent years, data has shown that seventy-four percent of the sex offenders who were incarcerated and in treatment in one prison were veterans of recent wars (Weldy and Associates, 1985).   It is not unreasonable to hypothesize that the act of witnessing or participating in (sexual) atrocities during the war predisposed at least some of these men to hostile and aggressive acts against women and children, a segment of the population perceived by them as being powerless.

Most authorities agree that it is extremely difficult to delineate the factors involved in sexually aggressive behavior, and some experts believe that the task is impossible.   Furthermore, many psychiatrists not only lack the ability to predict dangerousness of sex offenders, but they also lack the ability to properly evaluate their symptoms (Smith, 1965).

Psychiatrists differ in their definitions of abnormal and normal. Similarly, laws, values and attitudes regarding sexuality are often inconsistent and contradictory.   To further complicate matters, the topic of sexual deviation frequently elicits unconscious, primitive reactions.   On a conscious level, the topic may cause some people to express defensive and irrational responses.   If professionals are not aware of their own defensive and irrational responses to sexuality, their fears and conflicts, they, too, will be unable to remain dispassionate and unable to assess deviance with a needed degree of objectivity.

Unfortunately, many lay persons and professionals alike offer uninformed and dangerous opinions regarding the nature and effects of deviant behavior.   Therefore, besides coping with confused national values and monitoring professional responses to the sexuality of offenders, there is also a need to evaluate the evaluators: to be certain that the experts have a theoretical and factual foundation for their pronouncements.

The literature on sexuality and deviant sexuality contains innumerable examples of bias. Comfort (1972) considers lack of variety in sex (such as the exclusive use of the missionary position) a fetish. Bustanoby (1978) speaks of the provocative dress and seductive behavior of teenaged girls around their stepfathers. These stepfathers resist their stepdaughters' seductiveness which, in turn, lowers the girls' self esteem, with the result that the teens try harder to seduce their stepfathers to prove their own "sexual potency." Talent (1977) refers to exhibitionism/voyeurism as sometimes scary but not having lasting effects on its victims. He differentiates between nonconsenting and instigating victims of pedophiles and notes that we need to determine the type and degree of harm inflicted by the pedophile.

All of the reputable authorities in sexual abuse know that the psychological, emotional and sometimes physical damage inflicted by perpetrators can be devastating, and that the concept of consent is irrelevant when applied to minors. Therefore, legal or psychological professionals should be certain of the legitimacy of their sources of factual information.

Two studies illustrate the importance of consulting with knowledgeable professionals. Woods and Natterson (1967), after interviewing senior medical students, learned that a number of them believed that masturbation could cause mental illness, homosexuality, and impotence. Greenbank (1961) interviewed 540 interns and found that fifty percent believed that masturbation caused mental illness. Similarly, almost fifty percent experienced anxiety regarding general discussions of impotence, frigidity, sexual dysfunction in marriage, masturbation, and homosexuality.

An additional factor complicating the assessment process relates to the confused and contradictory nomenclature in regard to sexual deviation. In 1968 (American Psychiatric Assn., 1968), the DSM-II

(Diagnostic and Statistical Manual) stated that sexual deviation is not an appropriate diagnosis to apply to people who perform deviant sexual acts when normal sexual objects are not available to them. One wonders if this statement applied to all deviations. For what period of time were the "normal sexual objects" not available? Does not the nature and frequency of the deviation merit consideration?

Ellis, (1951) studying sexual attitudes, notes mass confusion both legally and morally. Added to the confusion is the fact that there are a number of proponents of eliminating sexual deviations from the psychiatric nomenclature. The proponents cite theories derived from Durkeim, Merton and Erikson on deviant adaptations. They view deviance as therapeutic to the individual and society, since deviance helps to maintain normative boundaries (Maris, 1971). Hence, deviations are viewed as potentially beneficial. If there is harm, it results from judging people as fit or unfit, in relation to a conformity to social norms. If the stigma is removed, the deviant may be better able to adjust and less likely to accept the self-fulfilling prophecy of permanence. Panzetta (1974) believes that there is a genuine danger in labeling because of this very illusion of permanence.

Other authorities question the ethics of legislating morality, the inherent conflict between conformity and self-determination (free will) and the problems of labeling deviants that result in coercive therapy. Finally, there are those professionals who question the very existence of mental illness (Szasz, 1965).

It is important to be aware of these various concerns that merit thoughtful consideration. Nonetheless, despite ideological, ethical, and legal confusions, professionals continue to attempt to evaluate those referred to as "deviant," and to treat those who are included in this very difficult to treat population.

Gathering Information

Client information and history forms are usually available in textbooks on psychiatric social work and counseling. These forms commonly include questions for gathering basic medical, emotional, psychological and historical data. Such information about sex offenders is important to obtain, along with copies of available police reports, probation and parole reports, criminal background checks, summaries and records from mental health clinics and agencies, and available information from child protective agencies.

In addition, collateral interviews with family members and close associates will also provide valuable information for the assessment. The nature of the clinical interview itself varies with its purpose. For example, to obtain information, the police must often be confronting and intimidating. In contrast, therapists working with sex offenders usually need to create an initial atmosphere of trust through a nonthreatening, nonconfronting approach. It is best not to question or confront the issue of denial or minimization during the first interview since confrontation will typically result in resistance. In addition, the initial interview need not focus solely on the sexual offense. The first objective is to build rapport and trust, and to set the stage for an in-depth, valid assessment.

Sexual Histories

A thorough questionnaire regarding sexuality and sexual issues constitutes an essential part of the assessment process for offenders. The questions should require thoughtful responses, responses that sometimes reveal the true character of the offender. An incest offender who describes his daughter as a "five-year-old femme fatale" reveals both regression and denial of responsibility for sexual abuse. Questions should help the interviewer to generate hypotheses about an offender's sexual aggressiveness in areas such as:

1) Delinquency (criminal, violent or antisocial orientation)— gleaned from a history of school difficulties, theft, chemical abuse and reported prior offenses;

2) Sexual satisfactions and dysfunctions—gleaned from specific questions on sexual practices and preferences;

3) Approaches to sexuality; the effects of, and attitudes associated with, sexuality—gleaned from questions regarding women, intimacy, home life and the work ethic;

4) Socialization and adaptive versus self-defeating behaviors —gleaned from work, marital and military history;

5) Impulse control; whether socialized behavior patterns stem from fear or guilt—gleaned from criminal history; interpersonal and vocational relationships;

6) Autonomy versus dependency needs—gathered from vocational history and interpersonal relations;

7) Ego-syntonic versus ego-alien behaviors—inferred from answers to questions related to guilt, remorse and victim empathy; and,

8) Specific aspects of sexual offenses, such as motives, methods, uses of coercion, frequency of behaviors and duration of deviant acts—noted in history and self-reports related to criminal actions.

Some of the information for the assessment will be obtained from the general history intake records. The rest should be obtained from questions in the sexual history. Special emphasis should be placed on the specific nature of past and present criminal sexual behavior. For each deviant act, determine:

1) Victim's age and sex

2) Age of offender at the time of the deviant act

3) Whether or not the act was intra- or extrafamilial

4) Type of act, i.e., intercourse (vaginal, anal), simulated intercourse, rape, cunnilingus, fellatio, fondling, exhibitionism, voyeurism, fetishism, forced to watch pornography

5) Duration and frequency

6) Presence of medical evidence

7) Use of threats, coercion, ritual, and weapons

8) Criminal disposition, if any.

Informal Assessment Instruments

Informal assessment tools, such as checklists and values clarification exercises, can be useful for gathering information and in formulating descriptive diagnoses. These tools also serve to help professionals formulate hypotheses regarding the problem areas to be explored during clinical interviews and ongoing therapeutic sessions.

Special instruments should be designed to elicit pertinent data from the sex offenders. Questions in the instruments should focus on deviant, aggressive or violent behavior, and should reveal such qualities as: defense mechanisms, proclivity toward acting-out behaviors, degree of moral development, past and present stresses, problem-solving skills, chemical abuse, communication skills, degree of social isolation/interaction and social-emotional-psychosexual adjustment. It is preferable to administer a variety of relatively brief questionnaires related to the above issues rather than lengthy ones. In addition, open-ended questions, or those requiring written responses of one or more sentences, often yield more useful information than scales or checklists.

Formal Testing

In general, the probability of recidivism is predicted more accurately by actuarial data on offenders' prior convictions than by psychiatric prognoses (Glaser, 1976; Glaser, 1962; Sawyer, 1966; Johns, 1967). As noted earlier, there are no demonstrably valid tests for predicting sexually deviant behavior. However, in developing an overall profile of sexually aggressive men, various factors should be considered. A standard battery of tests helps to complete the profile by providing information about educational skills and background, an intelligence quotient, personality factors and adjustment, and occupational aptitudes and abilities. Such a battery might include the following:

1) WAIS (Wechsler Adult Intelligence Scale) to measure education and intelligence;

2) 16 PF (16 Personality Factors) and MMPI (Minnesota Multiphasic Personality Inventory) to measure personality factors;[6]

3) GATB (General Aptitude Test Battery) to measure occupational skills; and,

4) WRAT (Wide Range Achievement Test) to measure reading, writing, spelling, and arithmetic skills.

To this list, the clinician might add the Rorschach, DAP (Draw-A-Person), and TAT (Thematic Apperception Test). While projective instruments lack reliability and validity, they may sensitize the therapist to themes and conflicts that otherwise might not be detected in standardized tests or through clinical interviews.

---

[6]Some authorities have found that adult sex offenders have elevated scores on the MMPI on the scales Psychopathic Deviate, Schizophrenia, and the Psychasthenia. Monachesi and Hathaway reported elevated MMPI scores on Psychopathic Deviate, Schizophrenia, and Hypomania in their sample of delinquents. Refer to: Monachesi, E.D., and Hathaway, G.R. "The Personality of Delinquents," in Buthcher, J.N. (Ed.), *MMPI: Research Developments and Clinical Applications.* New York: McGraw-Hill, 1969, 207-19. The implications for possible prevention and early detection of adolescent sex offenders are obvious.

Additional Assessment Tools

The Polygraph

There is considerable debate among criminologists, psychologists, polygraphers and scientists regarding the value of the lie detector test or polygraph. The instrument measures physiological responses or changes that occur under stressful conditions—pulse rate, blood pressure, rate and depth of breathing, and resistance of the skin to the conduction of electricity.

Authorities studying the polygraph cite several concerns regarding its validity:

1) Congress' Office of Technology Assessment (OTA) reviewed evidence regarding the polygraph. Leonard Saxe, director of the project, found six reviews of research recording accuracy rates from sixty-four to ninety-eight percent. Field studies recorded accuracy rates from seventy-five to ninety-seven percent (Joyce, 1984).

2) The American Polygraph Association cited studies yielding accuracy rates from 87.2% to 96.2 percent. One should note that these studies were conducted under laboratory conditions by psychologists and criminologists. (Meyer, 1984).

3) Psychologist David Lykken of the University of Minnesota, a critic of the polygraph, cited field studies yielding accuracy rates from sixty-four to seventy-one percent (Meyer, 1984).

Thus, statistical studies indicate that the polygraph is accurate from sixty-four to ninety-eight percent of the time. Meyer claims that, since the polygraph merely records emotional arousal and does not distinguish among emotions such as anxiety or guilt, it is not sufficiently valid or reliable. Meyer believes that the test results in more false positives (innocent people wrongly asserted to be guilty) than in guilty people concluded to be innocent (Meyer, 1984).

Furthermore, many other authorities believe that it is possible to defeat the polygraph. Smith states that a subject can focus on fantasies or tighten muscles to distract himself while being questioned. Moreover, honest, anxious subjects can be frightened into making false confessions. Smith notes that autonomic responses to unconscious attitudes can cause strong physiological reactions. Such reactions might be mistakenly interpreted as guilt and deception when, instead, they are merely rooted in anxiety (Smith, 1971).

Saxe stresses the importance of the examiner's skill in administering the polygraph, i.e., his or her manner of phrasing questions, ability to assess the respondent's tone of voice, and ability to detect deception. The room temperature, humidity and physical condition of the subject all affect the outcome of the test and mar its reliability (Smith, 1971).

In general, authorities concur that the ability to detect deceptive behavior varies widely. People differ in their sensitivity to stimuli, showing individual differences in responses to identical stressors. Some people may believe they are telling the truth when, in fact, they are deceiving themselves. In addition, some responses, thought to be under the control of the autonomic nervous system, are under voluntary control (Smith, 1971).

The consensus among many prominent researchers who have studied the use of the polygraph appears to be that the instrument lacks both validity and reliability; that statistics supporting its use generally have not been compiled by thorough independent investigations; and that it cannot be used as a part of a scientific technique since its use has not been based on sound scientific theory. Several researchers believe that there are ethical and moral issues to consider (Smith, 1984). Among these concerns is the fact that use of the polygraph may be termed voluntary, but refusal to submit to testing is often taken to imply deception on the part of the subject.

Narcoanalysis

Truth drugs can sometimes facilitate diagnosis and treatment, and are thought to be useful by some professionals in attempting to understand the etiology of deviant behavior. Repressed conflicts and traumas can be revealed under narcosis. Sodium amytal and sodium pentothal, the most commonly-used drugs in psychiatric sessions are easy to administer and provide somewhat predictable results. They are the least toxic and yield the least unfavorable side effects of the drugs in use.

However, it is commonly known that evidence derived from the use of truth drugs is inadmissable in court. This is because, even under narcosis, antisocial personalities have been known to deny crimes of which they have been guilty, while over-anxious patients have confessed to fantasized criminal activities. Hence, these drugs should not be relied upon to provide accurate results and should not be used in treatment (Freedman, 1971).

Pupillary Response

Measurements of the pupillary response to various stimuli, such as pornographic pictures of young children, have been used both to diagnose and assess the treatment progress of sex offenders. The rationale behind measuring pupil size is based on the fact that responses to visual stimuli vary from extreme dilation to pleasing material, to extreme constriction to distasteful material. Often, the clients' expressed verbal attitude regarding a given stimulus is at variance with his measured pupil response.

Hess (1971) noted that physiological factors can affect measurement. In other words, one does not know the effect that stress or anxiety may have on pupil response. Is it possible for an offender to visualize a different scene or picture from the one he is shown so that the measurement lacks accuracy? In addition, the equipment itself, such as the electrodes attached to the subject, may affect pupillary response.   Hence, the accuracy of using pupillary responses is of questionable value.

Single Gene Theory

Thirty years ago, researchers discovered an extra Y chromosome among a sample of imprisoned offenders. This discovery led to the popularization of the "XYY Syndrome" to explain male violence. The theory was soon discredited when it was found that the majority of the criminals with an extra Y chromosome were incarcerated for nonviolent offenses. The over-representation of the men with extra Y chromosomes in the prison population was explained by the fact that most of them had low intelligent quotients and were more likely to be apprehended than intelligent criminals (Baron, 1977).

Multiple Personality

In recent years, there has been new interest in the phenomenon of MPD (Multiple Personality Disorder). As a diagnosis, MPD has particular relevance to sex offenders who were victims of abuse, as well as to nonoffending victims of both sexes, and is stressed in this chapter because:

1)   Early childhood victimization/trauma can result in multiple personality;

2)   Multiple personality is a diagnosis with which many practitioners and case managers may be unfamiliar; and,

3)   It is important for professionals working with sex offenders to be aware of the relevance of MPD to their particular client population.

Recently, the American Psychiatric Association devoted two entire days of pre-conference workshops and two major symposia to the topic of MPD. Clearly, professionals are becoming more interested in, and concerned about, the seriousness of this psychiatric problem.

Victims of multiple personality disorder perceive themselves, or are perceived, as having two or more distinct personalities. Ninety-seven percent of MPD-afflicted individuals report histories of childhood trauma, mostly in the forms of physical, sexual or emotional abuse (Institute of Noetic Sciences, 1985).

Awareness of MPD is critically important for any therapist because eighty-nine percent of MPD's are not even aware of other personalities, and have been misdiagnosed at least once as depressed, borderline, epileptic, sociopathic, schizophrenic, or manic depressive personalities. Signs and symptoms of MPD include loss of time, blackouts, amnesia, self-destructive or suicidal behavior, sleep disorders, anorexia, somatic complaints, auditory or visual hallucinations, seizure-like episodes, depression and headaches (Institute of Noetic Sciences, 1985).

Those professionals interested in developing a deeper understanding of MPD may refer to:

Bliss, E.L. "Multiple Personalities: A Report of 14 Cases With Implications For Schizophrenia And Hypnosis," *Archives of General Psychiatry,* 37, December, 1980, 1388-97.

Cleckley, H. and Thigpen, C. *The Three Faces of Eve.* New York: McGraw Hill, 1957.

Greaves, G.B. "Multiple Personality 165 Years After Mary Reynolds," *Journal of Nervous and Mental Diseases,* 168 (10), October, 1980, 577-96.

Keyes, D. *The Minds of Billy Milligan.* New York: Bantam, 1981.

Schreiber, *F.R. Sybil.* New York: Warner, 1974.

From the foregoing, it is evident that additional assessment approaches and formal/informal tools are needed. Some of the assessment methods currently available are useful but lack empirical validity and precision.

Sex offenders have in common certain personality characteristics, defenses and coping mechanisms. An understanding and knowledge of the behavioral, emotional, and social traits of offenders facilitate both assessment and treatment.

Traits of Sex Offenders

* Compartmentalized feelings with little consideration of consequences for behaviors; do not easily self-correct or learn from experiences.

* Libidinize/sexualize relationships; hold sex stereotypes; often internalize madonna-whore complex regarding women.

* Limited world view and constricted behavioral-emotional repertoire; tend to deal in absolutes.

* Behave compulsively; tend toward addictions such as workaholic behavior or chemical abuse.

* Operate from self-centered, narcissistic and ego-centric orientation.

* Objectify others and lack empathic responses; relate superficially, viewing others as threatening to self-worth.

* Use various defenses such as denial, rationalization, minimization and projection of blame and responsibility.

* Suffer from conflicts centering around dependency-autonomy; are basically immature and impatient.

* Compensate for low self-worth by presenting selves as controlling, powerful and potent; see selves as failures who need to over-power others.

* Lack knowledge about interpersonal relationships, sexuality, male-female intimacy; lack trust of others.

* Lack self-control; have poor impulse control and low frustration tolerance; are oriented toward action rather than contemplation.

* Express anger violently or passive-aggressively; do not understand assertive behaviors or attitudes.

* Have poor communication skills.

* Adhere to rigid stereotypes regarding others; believe in segregated marriages with clear role divisions.

* Experience psychosexual identity problems; often are homophobic due to unresolved and latent homosexual impulses.

* Do not experience guilt or remorse for antisocial behaviors; need external controls for ego-syntonic acts or for uncontrolled ego-dystonic acts.

* Lack capacity for healthy conflict resolution.

* Lack social skills; often are withdrawn and isolated.

* Lie and manipulate to avoid blame and preserve self-image.

* Experience conflicts with real versus ideal self-image; have poor sense of self.

* Lack genuine commitments interpersonally and vocationally.

* Experience conflicts with authority.

Despite apparent progress in therapy, the sex offender is a very difficult client to treat. Case managers and therapists should be wary of their own naivety in assessing gains. It is wise to be aware of the fact that some offenders have a negative prognosis and remain at high risk, regardless of the intensity of therapeutic interventions. Factors contributing to poor-risk candidates for therapy include:

* Force or violence used during offenses (sexual and other); prior arrest record

* Bizarre rituals associated with offenses

* Polymorphous perversion and/or progressive deterioration evident from history of offenses

* Evidence of violent, acting-out behaviors

* Chronic chemical abuse

* Chronic high stressors in the environment

* Low I.Q./ capacity for insights

* History of severe childhood abuse

* Presence of persistent (paranoid, violent) fantasies

* General criminal lifestyle evident from history, background checks or prior arrests

* Offenses of fixation-compulsivity

* Sexual abuse of very young children

* Diagnosis of severe character disorder, paranoia, psychosis, retardation or organicity

* Persistence of defenses of denial and projection

* History of chronic social-sexual-maladaptation

* History of chronic vocational maladaption

* History of chronic sexual maladaption

* Community treatment providers and monitoring agents inadequate

To make gains in therapy, the offender must:

* Fully self-disclose and assume responsibility for behaviors

* Develop awareness and insights into the dynamics of offending behaviors

* Work through own early victimization

* Develop empathic skills

* Learn appropriate communication skills

* Obtain knowledge about sexuality and sex-role stereotyping

* Learn alternate anger and stress management techniques

* Improve self-image

* Develop a support system

* Stabilize employment

* Refrain from chemical abuse

* Learn to accept criticism and feedback

Relapses can be identified when the offender regresses in areas in which he has made gains, such as vocational and marital adjustment, stress management, social support system and chemical abuse.

Progress and Relapses

If the following factors are present, the sex offender in treatment has made gains and may be at relatively low risk for recidivist behavior:

* Low stress level

* Employment stability

* Lack of denial/rationalizations

* Victim-empathy

* Social support system

* Sexual adjustment with agemates

* Absence of serious psychopathology

* Nonviolent behaviors

* Anger management

* Adequate communication skills (assertiveness)

* Absence of chemical abuse

* Knowledge of the dynamics of abuse and high-risk situations

* Ability to express feelings

* Absence of deviant (especially violent or paranoid) fantasies

* Willingness to receive ongoing/periodic help

As is evident from this section, at best, the current approach to, and knowledge of, sex offenders is tentative at the very time when professionals are advocating the allocation of public funding for treatment and program expansion. Finding the answers and funding depends on the formulation of a deeper understanding of the dynamics of deviant behavior, the refinement of the diagnostic tools presently in use, the development of new test measures, and the conduct of empirical research on the nature and etiology of sex offenses.

At present, there are no accurate measures to predict sexually aggressive behavior. The checklists for indicating high-risk candidates for recidivism are informal. Besides lacking the ability to distinguish among the types of offenders—predatory child molesters, criminal psychopaths, and regressed perpetrators—professionals are also unable to make reliable expert distinctions between treatable and nontreatable perpetrators.

What is known at the present time is that:

1)   The likelihood of recidivism tends to decrease with age;

2)   Chemical abuse adversely affects parole performance;

3)   The most useful predictive device relative to recidivism is past criminal behavior;

4)   Statistical devices are more accurate predictors than interviews; and,

5)   All current available methods have relatively low predictive power (Gottfredson, 1977).

Case Histories

The importance of careful assessment is illustrated in the following case histories.   In the three cases summarized below, the information gathering process was hasty and inadequate, leading to inappropriate treatment recommendations.

John, a thirty-one-year-old married man, sexually abused his eleven-year-old natural daughter for approximately one year. Offenses included fondling, cunnilingus and attempted vaginal intercourse. John admitted incestuous abuse following his daughter's disclosure. A background check indicated that there were no prior arrests and the family was screened into group therapy in Parents United.

In private therapy, John admitted to having a lengthy history of sexually deviant behavior. At the age of twelve, he had stood on the fire-escape of his parent's apartment building and watched through a window as his father raped his sister. While watching, he had an erection and masturbated to climax. Thereafter, John became a compulsive voyeur. In addition, at age ten, he had been sexually assaulted by the father of one of his friends.

From mid-adolescence into his late twenties, he had a number of homosexual experiences, often with boys under eighteen. Probably for reassurance of his masculinity and to demonstrate his hostility toward women, John participated in the gang rape[7] of a number of teenage females and adult women during his adolescence.

Thus, John manifested polymorphous sexually aggressive behavior, including voyeurism, homosexuality, homosexual abuse of minors, gang rape, and incestuous abuse. The initial descriptive diagnosis of regressed incest offender clearly was inaccurate. Hence, the treatment plan involving Parents United, a group therapy program for regressed incest offenders, was inappropriate and John's prognosis was guarded at best.

Distrustful of the system, John was careful in making initial disclosures. He knew that honesty would result in a possible prison term. In addition, the screening process by the police, county attorney, probation officer, and social workers at Parents United was perfunctory. Several of the professionals involved in that screening process had little experience working with sex offenders. As is often the case, John's self-reporting was perceived as honest, despite the fact that he was character-disordered and heavily invested in avoiding imprisonment.

Two other men, also labeled incest offenders, both sexually abused their three-year-old natural daughters for approximately one year. In each case, digital fondling of the genitals, fellatio and cunnilingus were involved.

Each offender appeared to be anally fixated, focusing aspects of the abuse on defecation. In one situation, the child was forced to defecate on her father and to lick feces from his penis; in the other, the child was forced to defecate in the bed where the abuse

---

[7]In addition, often there is a component of homosexual gratification in *gang rape*.

occurred and to endure frequent enemas. Cruel, sadistic and ritualistic elements were evident in both abuse cases. Neither of these men was a fixated pedophile or regressed offender. Their behavior was criminally psychopathic. As in many situations involving sexually abused infants, there were elements of copraphilia and fetishism.

For all client populations, assessment precedes diagnosis and diagnosis is essential in the formulation of appropriate treatment strategies. Too often, hasty assessment procedures lead to improper diagnoses and the resultant treatment approaches are ineffectual. For sex offenders, the need for precision in assessment and diagnosis is especially important because of the threat this criminal population poses to the safety of others.

4

DANGERS OF DENIAL

Rape is the having of carnal knowledge of a woman forcibly and against her will. Sexual intercourse with a child under the age of consent fixed by law, with an insane woman, or a woman in a condition in which she cannot consciously consent, or when consent is extorted by fear, is rape, though no actual force be used (Fishback, 1896).

The above legal and therapeutic definition of rape has not changed substantially since 1896 when Fishback's text was published. However, humanists in the 1970's, starting perhaps with Brownmiller (1975), and encouraged by the rise of feminism, have had an impact on societal norms and the law. Today, many people realize that the absence of consent (not the presence of force) is the key determinant in assessing whether or not rape has occurred. In the last few years, the media also has performed a major service by increasing public awareness about the epidemic of child sexual abuse. Finally, since the late 1970's, conscientious and dedicated professionals have been accumulating a body of anecdotal, clinical and data-based research supporting the following facts:

1)   Children rarely lie when disclosing child sexual abuse (Goodwin, et. al., 1980).

2)   Young child victims are incapable of participating in an adversarial court process.

3)   Legal procedures for adult and child victims require major reforms to prevent re-victimization by the judicial system.

4)   Victims suffer from Child Sexual Abuse Syndrome and Rape Trauma Syndrome which add to the reliability of their disclosure and discredit notions of their consent and fabrication.[7]

5)   Child victims often recant initial disclosures due to various fears and pressures.[8]

6)   Perpetrators typically deny their offenses.

Progressive changes in attitudes and behaviors have come slowly, and yet, these changes represent hope that contemporary legal theory and practices will continue to advocate a humanitarian approach to victimization. Unfortunately, however, change is threatening to those groups that believe public awareness has become pervaded with lunatic fervor and that nationally-publicized child

---

[7]Rape Trauma Syndrome has been well-documented in the literature since the mid-1970's. Refer to: Burgess, A.W., and Holmstrom, L.L. "Rape Trauma Syndrome," *Nursing Digest,* May-June 1975, 17-18. Dr. Roland Summit, Head Physician and Associate Professor of Psychiatry, Harbor UCLA Medical Center, Torrance, CA, is a leading authority on child sexual abuse. He has written extensively on the Child Sexual Abuse or Accommodation Syndrome as well as on recantation and fabrication related to disclosures.

[8]Many authorities attest to the fact that offenders use denial as a primary defense. Refer to: Bulkley, J.(ED.). *Innovations in the Prosecution of Child Sexual Abuse Cases.* Washington, DC: American Bar Association, National Legal Resource Center for Child Advocacy and Protection, November, 1981, 44.

sexual abuse scandals in Minnesota and California in the mid-1980's represent veritable witch hunts fomented to destroy innocent families.

VOCAL (Victims of Child Abuse Laws) is one group that was organized in Minnesota in October, 1984. Since its formation, it has become a nonprofit organization that currently has 3000 members and a number of chapters throughout Minnesota as well as in more than thirty other states.

In their report to the Minnesota Attorney General in 1984, VOCAL members identified themselves as parents who believe they have been victimized by child abuse laws. They claim that they want to have their children protected from all forms of abuse— including abuse perpetrated by child protective agencies. VOCAL advocates that, whenever feasible, the states should protect the family unit in managing child abuse cases.

The specific concerns and complaints of VOCAL members, as outlined in their report to the Attorney General, included the following:

1)   Immediate presumption of guilt for the accused in abuse cases;

2)   Biased investigation;

3)   Use of opinions by mental health professionals in legal proceedings;

4)   Abrupt removal of children from the home;

5)   Stigma and financial burden on families under investigation; and,

6)   Dependency petitions filed to make children wards of the state after charges of neglect and abuse have been dropped.

In the same report, members suggested possible alternatives and solutions to their grievances. Their suggestions included the following:

1) VOCAL members be allowed to participate in task forces on child abuse and neglect;

2) All family members be interviewed following allegations of abuse to check the reliability and credibility of alleged child victims;

3) The alleged perpetrator be removed from the home, not the child;

4) Parents be allowed to find placements for their children rather than have them removed by the state;

5) Training for social workers be improved and include yearly tests concerning updated child abuse laws and guidelines;

6) Child protective service agencies be mandated to allow children to remain in their homes when situations are not life-threatening and there is no substantiation of sexual/ physical abuse or neglect;

7) Taping of all interviews be mandated and available to defense attorneys; and,

8) Exclude expert opinions by social workers.

Other groups have organized since the formation of VOCAL, among them, The Family Rites Coalition in Crystal Lake, Illinois, which serves as a clearinghouse for information regarding "unjust aggression" by government agencies. Articles, pamphlets, and statistical reports are being compiled by these groups to counteract the alleged state takeover of the family and usurpation of parental rights and privileges. One recent article quotes Margretta Dwyer, R.S.M., M.A., University of Minnesota Medical School, who claims that approximately seventy percent of divorce cases with allegations of child molestation are hoaxes. Dwyer further believes that books that focus on good and bad touching are harmful for children because of the terminology used (Bulkley, 1981).

In general, the literature supporting these groups is anecdotal, hypothetical, and argumentative. Distortions and generalizations abound. Abused children are said to invite abuse. Emotionally disturbed children are characterized as liars. Recommendations support parental, not children's, rights. It is suggested that a child victim's history be thoroughly checked to establish credibility. Parents, on the other hand, need only provide character references of their choosing to attest to their veracity.

Jones (1985) criticizes attempts to reform antiquated court procedures that further victimize children. He opposes videotaping children's testimony as a manipulative device along with the introduction of hearsay testimony in court proceedings. Believing that defendants are not protected and that there is a feminist conspiracy attacking the integrity of the traditional family, Jones reports that therapists are exploiting and creating family pathology for personal gains related to finances and status. Therapists and prosecutors are likened to funding parasites who gain recognition and increased earnings by exploiting child sexual abuse. Jones even accuses therapists of competing with natural parents by becoming the advocates and protectors of the children.

VOCAL supporters also criticize the allocation of state monies for the prevention of child sexual abuse, citing invasion of privacy in the classroom as one of the inevitable by-products of educational efforts to decrease victimization (Jones, 1985). The good faith clause, operable in many states and exempting from civil lawsuits any professional who reports suspected abuse, is condemned as an additional tactic that violates family privacy. The extremist rhetoric of these writers exacerbates existing fears among people who are intimidated by authority, with constant, exaggerated references to the sweeping powers of state and government agencies bent on destroying innocent, unsuspecting families.

Much of the rhetoric of extremist writers is emotional, with limited or no logical or factual basis. For example, child protective agencies following strict state guidelines traditionally have advocated the preservation of the family unit whenever possible in abuse cases. Children are removed only as a last resort when mothers and other relatives are perceived as nonprotecting and nonsupportive. Mothers sometimes blame child victims for incestuous abuse. They and other relatives do influence children to recant initial-disclosures in order to maintain the status quo financially and emotionally.

In general, children are more likely to be believed when they report child abuse because the data from experts in the field corroborates the fact that young victims rarely lie about child sexual abuse. More often than not, children fail to disclose intrafamilial molestation for fear of the innumerable repercussions they will suffer from family members if they do disclose (Whitfield, 1985).

The growth of movements to counter humane efforts on behalf of victims is both frightening and dangerous. Members of VOCAL and similar groups appeal to the emotions of their audiences, partly by invoking traditions and values related to pride in individualism and the sanctity of the home.

Additional danger exists in that some of the arguments couched within an overall specious approach do, in fact, merit attention. Child protective agencies do need more training for their caseworkers, and the indiscriminate use of therapists at various levels of competency as experts is unconscionable. Abuses do, in fact, exist and a number of innocent men and women inevitably suffer from injustices inherent in an imperfect system.

Therapists need to be aware of the potential power of the critical organizations, partly to avoid emotional counter-reactions. These groups may well grow in numbers and influence.

During November, 1985, for example, VOCAL held its first national conference with featured speakers including Douglas Besharov, J.D., first director of the National Center for Child Abuse, and State Senator Wegscheid (D.MN.). With prominent speakers and a three-day agenda, the conference highlighted the growing significance of VOCAL as a powerful political force.

Publications with bogus statistics may find their way into court-rooms via a new breed of experts-for-hire by defense attorneys. Legislators, lacking knowledge about abuse, may be influenced by the appeals to preserve individual and family rights. Hence, it is incumbent upon legislators and experienced professionals to remain accountable, credible and objective. Arguments should be based on factual information derived from adequate clinical and research samples. Equally, it is important for human service professionals to monitor their own zealous reactions, not only with regard to the treatment of sex offenders, but also with regard to the treatment of victims.

In uncovering sex scandals involving children, for example, we need to be certain that we follow clear and established guidelines on interviewing children as well as observe due process regarding all legal proceedings. The doubts surrounding the existence of sexual abuse in recent scandals in Minnesota and California, point to the need for competent media management and a cautious, conservative approach by the professional community. As a result of the emphasis by the media on the exploitation of the accused and the workings of the legal system, the focus of attention does not tend to be directed toward alleged child victims and their needs.

It seems evident that in an area as damaging as sexual abuse/assault, every possible precaution is needed to ensure restitution in its various forms, including the criminal prosecution of perpetrators and the correct, legal and humane management of victims. To err in these matters means the loss of credibility with the victims, their advocates and the tax-paying public. Failure may result in the delay or cessation of needed prevention and treatment programs, to the detriment of everyone.

5

THE COURT PROCESS

The criminal justice system often inadvertently revictimizes survivors of intrafamilial and extrafamilial sexual abuse and rape. Revictimization occurs primarily through court delays and multiple interviews of the victims. In addition, the system also fails to discriminate among the treatable and nontreatable. Likewise, the system antagonizes the population at large which is becoming frustrated with increased reports of sexual molestation and rape, and with evidence of rising recidivism rates among sex offenders at large.

Glaser (1976) reports that the policing, charging and sentencing of sex offenders are among the most haphazard and biased acts in the criminal justice system. He cites a number of reasons for the seemingly arbitrary behavior of the courts, including: only a few (of the many) cases are actually reported for legal review, and the court's dependency on both lay and expert persons who may have only a limited understanding of sexually aggressive acts. Two aspects of the legal apparatus bear examination: 1) the approaches of the criminal justice system to child molesters and rapists, and 2) the effects of the adjudication process on victims and their advocates.

Child Molesters

Recently, in Phoenix, Arizona, a man convicted for the third time of passing a stopped school bus received a sentence of six months incarceration along with a fine of $1000.00. Compare his penalty with the following disillusioning statistics regarding the legal consequences to forty-five longtime incestuous offenders and pedophiles.

Consequences	Number of Men
Never apprehended	4
Apprehended but not charged.	11
Charged, convicted, placed on probation with no jail time	3
Charged, convicted, placed on probation with thirty days or less jail plus work release	7
Charged, convicted, placed on probation with three to six months jail plus work release	5
Charged, convicted, placed on probation with nine to twelve months jail plus work release	8
Charged, convicted, sent to prison	2
Pending	4
(Suicide)	1

Of the forty living offenders whose cases were not pending, eighteen received no legal penalties for their offenses; and twenty-five, or well over half, received either no penalties or sentences of thirty days or less of incarceration/work release. Forty-three of the forty-five men were classified as incest offenders; two as pedophiles, and three as exhibitionists/voyeurs.

Three of the incest offenders, however, had committed rapes, and one admitted to murdering three men years earlier. In therapy, the two pedophiles admitted to having sexually abused at least 175 children. One of these men received a sentence of thirty days with work release, plus probation; the second has never been apprehended. The forty-three incest offenders claimed to have molested a total of ninety-two children. This sample did not include a number of offenders who were interviewed but not in therapy, nor did it include any offender of children under the age of five. Often, children under five are not considered legally competent to testify. Therefore, it is rare to encounter a sex offender who will admit to the molestation of very young children. He need not admit his crime because he knows that the courts are not able to prove his guilt (Glaser, 1976).

As is evident from the statistics above, a number of the offenders attended therapy and worked at their jobs even while incarcerated for short-terms in the county jail. Without exception, these men referred to jail as "Club Med," or vacation-time. In jail, their lives were free of stress while in their homes, their wives shouldered the emotional burdens of coping with the children and maintaining a semblance of family life.

There are several reasons underlying the imposition of lenient sentences on incest offenders and pedophiles. First are the arguments against lengthy mandated sentences posed by legislators, state planners and professional experts. One of the more cogent arguments centers around the fear that since eighty-five percent of child molestation is intrafamilial, lengthened sentences will result in a reduction in reported cases. The threat of incarceration will prompt incest offenders and their victims to keep the last taboo a family secret.

In addition, it is feared that if juries know that sentences will be harsh, they will be reluctant to believe child victims and/or to convict guilty offenders.

A second rationale for short-term sentences has been predicated on the premature notion that offenders are, in fact, treatable, and that therapists currently understand how to treat them effectively. In some instances, mental health professionals appear to be advocating therapy in the admitted absence of proven treatment methodologies. Recently, for example, Arizona held a statewide conference and call to action in the face of rising reports of sex crimes. The conference, resulted in a draft of a number of policy recommendations for the state legislature. One recommendation called for mandated, "specialized treatment for all sex offenders." This recommendation for treatment, ironically, referred to our current knowledge of effective treatment as, "incomplete and inconclusive," leading us to be "less than enthusiastically optimistic about treatment." The recommendation further included a call for uniform, standardized assessment and evaluation of sex offenders without consideration of, or reference to, the availability, type, source or nature of the advocated testing.

The notion of treatability can be attributed, in large part, to the proliferation of community-based, incest-family treatment programs modeled after Parents United in San Jose, California (Parents United, 1985). Parents United now boasts of over 150 chapters internationally, and claims that the recidivism rate among father-offenders treated in the program is less than one percent (Parents United, 1985).

Many professionals believe that community-based treatment for incestuous families offers a number of advantages over either incarceration or traditional therapeutic interventions. However, since the inception of Parents United in 1971, longitudinal studies on success rates are not yet available. Moreover, three variables mar the validity of existing studies. First, cost-effectiveness resulting from the removal of sex offenders from the home while maintaining abused children in the family, offers a significant incentive for legislators and state planners to promote a program that saves taxpayers countless dollars formerly used to subsidize foster care and residential placement for child victims. Second, reporting rates depend not only on re-arrest data, but also on self-disclosures by offenders. The vast majority of incest offenders initially deny their offenses and only rarely self-report. Thus, it is unlikely that these offenders would report recidivist behavior, especially since re-arrest might well result in long-term imprisonment. Finally, child victims, having already suffered from the humiliations and frustrations resulting from initial disclosures, are not likely to report recidivist behavior by their fathers or stepfathers.

On a national level, the criminal approach to incestuous offenders has been setting a dangerous precedent. There is a pronounced need to re-evaluate the ethical and legal positions regarding victimization in the home. Sentencing incestuous offenders should be consistent and based on an honest assessment of potential treatability. An inter-disciplinary, cooperative liaison between the legal system and treat-ment providers might help to minimize the devastating effects of the currently unjust and inequitable approach to incest offenders.

Often, this approach is haphazard, resulting in wide discrepancies in sentencing. One offender may be sentenced to years of imprison-ment while another, charged with the same or a similar offense, accepts a plea bargain, and receives a sentence of short-term jail, work furlough and probation.

Finally, each state should have a videotape statute allowing children's testimony to be filmed for use in trial to balance the defendant's right to face his accuser with the child's right to be protected.

Rapists

A well-publicized case, reported in Newsweek's issue of May 20, 1985, involved twenty-eight-year-old Gary Dotson, convicted in 1979 of the 1977 rape of then sixteen-year-old Cathleen Crowell Webb in a Chicago suburb. Eight years after the alleged crime occurred, the victim recanted her disclosure of rape.

The Dotson case set off fears among victim advocates throughout the nation that reforms in the treatment of rape victims by the criminal justice system would be adversely affected for years to come. It is interesting that the position with reference to victimization is still so tenuous that the fear aroused by a single recantation will cast doubt upon the credibility of countless females who have suffered rape.

Until the early 1970's, coincident with the publication of Susan Brownmiller's *Against Our Will*, rape victims suffered shame, frustration, and humiliation from the medical and therapeutic community as well as from the courts. The male prerogative to treat females as sexual objects, coupled with the fear of unfair allegations, established a social climate in which any victim was treated as the guilty party. A woman's credibility was in doubt; her sexual history was questioned; her consent was assumed; and her testimony required corroboration. In some states, judges were mandated to tell jurors that women sometimes lied regarding allegations of rape.

Today, about forty states have enacted reform legislation, including the elimination of: the demand for proof of physical resistance by victims, the need for corroborative testimony, proof of penetration and/or the presence of semen, and the admissibility of the past sexual histories of victims.

Hospitals have personnel trained to deal specifically with rape victims. Staff physicians, sensitive to the needs of victims, perform standardized sexual assault examinations designed to minimize physical and emotional trauma. Nationwide, many of our police forces have established training programs for officers assigned to sexual assault units and, in a number of cities, female officers conduct initial investigations in suspected rape cases (Newsweek, 1985).

These reforms have resulted in increased reporting rates. Since 1960, rape reports have tripled; since 1970, they have doubled. Rape arrests now yield convictions in nineteen percent of the cases instead of the ten percent of a decade ago (Newsweek, 1985).

Despite these reforms, women still perceive rape as their problem, one to be solved by self-defense for victims rather than punishment for offenders. In the mid-1970's, Burgess (1976) and Holmstrom identified a cluster of short- and long-term symptoms commonly suffered by rape victims and now known as Rape Trauma Syndrome (RTS). Recognition of RTS, acknowledged by the therapeutic but not the legal, community, clearly counters the notion of consent.

A consenting partner does not suffer from symptoms including nightmares, phobias, sexual dysfunction, psychogenic problems, social withdrawal, changes in appetite, insomnia, feelings of helplessness, anger, fear of being alone and the like. Consenting partners do not feel the need to move from their neighborhoods and change jobs following rape. Nonetheless, a number of symptoms accompanying Rape Trauma Syndrome, including guilt, shame and humiliation, lend credence to the prevalence of self-blame among victims.

Victims not only contend with self-victimization in the form of self-blame, but also must deal with the reality of slow-developing and inadequate reforms in rape legislation. Every survey indicates under-reporting of rape, typically by one-half. Moreover, in cases where victims know the offenders (and one-third of all assaults are classified as acquaintance rapes) convictions are hard to obtain. Finally, spousal rape remains difficult to prosecute, even in those states (twenty-five states and Washington D.C.) where it has been recognized as a crime. Only one hundred cases of spousal rape have been prosecuted and most of these cases involved couples who were separated.

If the current legal and social climate persists, rape victims will continue to avoid bringing their cases to the criminal justice system, where, at best, they anticipate revictimization, and, at worst, they perceive that offenders receive little, if any, punishment. In reality, the majority of rapists suffer no consequences for their crimes. Most rapists are not caught, and, if they are apprehended, many of them are not formally charged. If charged, most of them are not convicted. For those who are convicted, incarceration rarely exceeds a few years.

Until the orientation toward the crime of rape changes radically, one cannot expect victims to assist in the apprehension and prosecution of offenders.   In the interim, both victims and treatable sex offenders will suffer from bias, prejudice and inequitable treatment from both criminal authorities and the public.

Incest Victims

Kee MacFarlane (1985), a California expert on child sexual abuse, commenting on a sexual abuse scandal in a preschool, noted that child witnesses were terrified by the court experience and that their emotional scars resulting from the trial would last for years. Each witness faced as many as six defense attorneys, sometimes for time periods of up to fifty hours in a span of two weeks.   Many of the children developed symptoms resulting not from alleged victimization but, rather, from the repeated, unmerciful badgering by defense attorneys.

A related story described the trial of a foster father charged with seven counts of molestation and causing great bodily injury to his ten-year-old foster daughter (People, July 8, 1985).   During what is described as excruciating testimony, the child witness was harassed and accused of fabrication and fantasizing, despite medical evidence indicating the presence of sperm and vaginal bleeding following one assault, a ruptured and scarred hymen, and internal vaginal injuries.

The defense attorney in this case acknowledged his skill at incriminating child witnesses, a skill he claimed to have honed, in part, by attending seminars sponsored by the Los Angeles County Public Defender's Office where attorneys are systematically instructed on methods to confuse, intimidate and frighten child witnesses.   The defendant in the above case was found guilty on all counts and received a sentence of twenty years imprisonment.

These courtroom practices, hardly uncommon, clearly constitute inhumane practices.   Expert witnesses, subpoenaed to testify on behalf of child victims, recount horror stories in which both they and their young clients feel abused, harassed, badgered and humiliated, as they attempt to face hostile defendants and defense attorneys, often indifferent prosecutors, inexperienced judges, and juries unfamiliar with the prevalence of molestation, the credibility of children, and the Child Sexual Abuse Syndrome.[9]

District Attorney, Robert "Bud" Cramer, who heads the Children's Advocacy Center in Huntsville, Alabama, eloquently recounts the trauma suffered by child-victim witnesses who testify in court. Revictimized by the system, children are subjected to repeated "quizzes" by as many as seven to ten different strangers before they are required to testify in court. Cramer notes that by the time victims reach the D.A.'s office, many refuse to talk at all.[10]

The sexualizing of the adversarial female-victim versus male-defendant court process merely exacerbates existing problems. In addition, defense attorneys, often doubting the innocence of the clients whom they represent, appear to use the defense mechanisms

---

[9]On numerous occasions, I have testified in criminal courts as an expert witness on child sexual abuse. I came to understand that the judicial system desperately needs education and reform. I listened as one defense attorney stated that his client was not guilty because he "looked heterosexually competent" and another asserted that he loved law because he "needed to fuck people." Following a finding guilty against his client, a third defense attorney alleged that he, not the victim, "was raped in court."

[10]To minimize the court trauma for children, the Children's Advocacy Center in Huntsville, Alabama, was established two years ago linking prosecutors, police, social workers, medical personnel and other professionals. Cramer's office now boasts a sixty to seventy percent conviction rate. Reported by Randy Quarles, Times Washington correspondent, in the Huntsville Times, "DA Cramer Tells of Difficulties Sex Victims Face," May 3, 1985.

of rationalization, identification and reaction formation as they become overzealous and vehement advocates for the accused.

In open court, children are referred to as liars, bad seeds, and manipulators. Ridiculously implausible explanations are presented to ignorant juries in order to cast doubt upon the occurrence of abuse. Children suffering from rectal lax tone and vaginal enlargement due to what reputable physicians claim is penile penetration, are accused of self-mutilation with the use of coke bottles and sticks. Children who compulsively masturbate are said to be suffering from generalized anxiety related to any cause other than sexual abuse.

Sexual abuse is quantitated and the Child Sexual Abuse Syndrome is compartmentalized, so that single symptoms such as apathy and depression become the focus for interminable cross-examination with the intent of proving multiple or unknown causation. Experts are accused of relying on the facile bromide that "children do not lie." Clearly, in no other area of behavioral health are we demanding such a degree of scientific proof for alleged events. If it cannot be proven "to a medical certainty" that a child alleging molestation, had, in fact, been sexually abused, then it is assumed that the child is fabricating.

Seemingly, the so-called witch hunt for sexual offenders has been reversed. Now, it is the victims whom we seek to discredit. One wonders if victim-advocates are correct in their observation that unless changes occur, under present circumstances, adults legally are entitled to use children as sexual objects and playthings for any imaginable form of abuse.

It is true that the publicity associated with child sexual abuse has created a furor of skepticism regarding the credibility of children, particularly in custody cases. Nevertheless, there are currently no longitudinal studies on fabrication in custody or other cases, even though some professionals hypothesize that mothers may coach children to falsely accuse fathers of molestation in order to win custody battles. Teenagers, also, are not universally believed. Again, the absence of data on fabrication among adolescents leads to mere speculation regarding their credibility.

Children in the latency age group often are believed by therapists and prosecutors, and they can present themselves as credible, strong witnesses. Yet, it is this age group that often risks the most by disclosing abuse. Children between the ages of six and eleven are old enough to realize the consequences of their reports: possible family disruption and retaliations against them, economic hardship and court involvement. In addition, they are too young and dependent upon the nuclear unit to envision survival in the face of parental rejection. Hence, recantation is common among prepubescent youngsters.

As noted earlier, children under the age of five receive scant attention from the criminal justice system. Finally, sexually victimized children, among all age groups, lose credibility if they manifest the very symptoms that characterize molested youngsters: manipulation, overt promiscuity/seductiveness, a capacity for lying, emotional instability and other behavioral problems.

Despite the numerous problems related to children's credibility, professionals generally believe victims. Data regarding the veracity of children are anecdotal, but clinical reports by experienced experts indicate that fabrication is the exception, not the rule. Moreover, we are now beginning to compile a body of literature exploring the many facets of children's memory (Goodman, 1984).

Goodman and Michelli report that adults are biased against children's testimony and, yet, children do recall events accurately if they are not confused or intimidated by adults. Moreover, children can meet the test of competency. The authors describe a 1979 study by Barbara Marin, Deborah Holmes and others at Loyola University in Chicago which indicates that children make fewer inaccurate statements than adults. In general, there is no more reason to believe adults than children. Despite these reasons, jurors still remain biased against child witnesses. This finding is particularly interesting in view of the following facts:

1) Children rarely benefit emotionally, psychologically, or legally from disclosing abuse. For this reason, they usually suffer for years before reporting molestation. They fear the consequences of disclosure and often report abuse only when they feel desperate and unable to find alternate solutions. Therefore, they lack motivation to fabricate.

2) Offenders, on the other hand, typically are character-disordered and quite capable of lying and manipulating. Generally, they deny their offenses, at least initially. Their motivation to lie is obvious.

A final issue regarding child witnesses merits attention. Once child sexual abuse is reported, the victim becomes a witness for the state. The prosecutor's primary goal is to win the case. Thus, child victims, unlike their abusers, do not have legal representation. Their competence and credibility are questioned, and they are at the mercy of an adversarial system established for adults. At the very least, child sex abuse experts should serve as impartial consultants and trainers for judges, prosecutors and juries. Clearly, there is a desperate need to develop reforms for the humane protection of children.

Rape Victims

Women who have been sexually assaulted suffer from consequences similar to those of child victims of sexual abuse. During November, 1984, the American Psychological Association completed a two-year study on victims of violent crimes which, among other findings, concluded that society invests heavily in the accused and not in the victim who is traumatized by callous inattention. The report further states that laws often exacerbate the psychological impact of victimization. Victims in criminal cases feel isolated and uninformed about the investigation of their cases because they become witnesses for the state, i.e., "pieces of evidence" (Bard, 1980).

Feminists and other victim-advocates have published a variety of articles that enhance victim empathy and highlight the ludicrous inconsistencies in our approach to female rape victims versus other victims of violent crime. For example, if a woman is robbed on the street, she is not asked by the authorities what she was wearing, why she was walking alone, or if she had been robbed before. She does not have to prove resistance or loss of funds. It is irrelevant to the legal system that the victim wore expensive clothing at the time of the crime. If the robber is apprehended, he is not given preferential treatment by the courts.

On September 26, 1985, the *Arizona Republic* reported on a two-year sociological study of jurors from thirty-eight contested rape cases in Indianapolis. The lifestyles of rape victims affect decisions by the jury, i.e., jurors tend to believe married women assaulted in their homes behind locked doors, whereas black women, single women and mothers of children without identifiable fathers lack credibility (Psychology Today, October 1985). University of Illinois sociologist Barbara Reskin notes that jurors are affected by the personal characteristics of defendants as well as by those of victims. For example, attractive men with access to sexual partners are not perceived as being capable of rape (Sweet, 1985).

In addition to having to contend with an impersonal, unsympathetic system with biased jurors, the rape victim faces an array of legal maneuvers and tactics by defense attorneys and prosecutors alike. In one case, a prosecutor did not plan to object to anticipated, ruthless cross-examination of a fifteen-yearold rape victim by the defense attorney. His rationale involved an attempt to elicit juror sympathy for a victim he knew was fragile and cried profusely when forced to discuss the brutal assault which left her thoroughly traumatized. Also, psychological research is being applied to jury selection to ensure member bias, despite the fact that the 6th Amendment guarantees the right to an impartial jury (Andrews, 1982).

While it is difficult to prove violent rape in the American court-room, it appears to be almost impossible to obtain convictions in cases involving acquaintance or date rape.

Martha Burt, director of the Social Services Research Center at the Urban University in Washington, D.C., contends that there is a "rape supportive belief system" in the United States, a large segment of the population that fosters and believes in myths about rape. These myths include the belief that women lie about rape; that rape does not really exist; that if rape does exist, it causes no harm; and that women deserve or provoke whatever happens to them (Sweet, 1985).

The fact that a part of society appears to be entrenched in denial regarding acquaintance rape is a truly unfortunate phenomenon since sixty to eighty percent of rapes are perpetrated by men who know their victims (Callaway). MS Magazine's Campus Project on Sexual Assault involved a two-year study on rape directed by Mary P. Koss at Kent State University, funded by the National Center for the Prevention and Control of Rape. Thirty-five schools and 7000 students were involved in this study, the results of which were published in the October, 1985 issue of MS, (p.58).

The study presented the following findings:

1)   Fifty-two percent of the sample of women had been sexually victimized.

2)   One in every eight females in the sample had been a victim of rape.

3)   One in every twelve men had attempted or committed rape.

4)   Forty-seven percent of the rapes were acquaintance or date rapes.

5) More than one-third of the women raped did not disclose the assault to anyone; more than ninety percent did not report the rape to the police.

Compounding legal problems and cultural bias is the unfortunate fact that women who have experienced date or acquaintance rape are more likely to blame themselves than are the victims of other violent crimes. Victims of date or acquaintance rape tend to internalize prevailing social beliefs and experience severe guilt which often exacerbates the other symptoms of Rape Trauma Syndrome. These women usually do not have, nor seek, the minimal support and validation offered to brutalized victims of other crimes.

The plight of the rape victim merits serious and immediate social and legal consideration. Until victims are validated psychologically, emotionally, socially and legally, they will continue to suffer in alienated silence.

PART II:

MANAGEMENT AND TREATMENT APPROACHES

6

AN ETHICAL DILEMMA:
Treatment or Punishment

To single out the sex offender for rehabilitation implies the likelihood that he is treatable. However, a review of the current literature clearly reveals that this conclusion is not based on valid evidence. Many authorities cite the lack of substantive data on the effects of the legal versus the therapeutic approaches to the management of sex offenders, yet, treatment programs within and outside of the prison settings, while still not proportionate to the number of sex offenders, have proliferated in recent years.

The first four treatment programs for sex offenders in the United States were established in California (1948), in Wisconsin (1951), and in Massachusetts and Washington (both 1958). By 1984, Knopp provided a noninclusive listing of 197 specialized adult sex offender treatment programs offered by agencies and individuals.

In the 1930's and 1940's, sex offenders were perceived as victims of hereditary defects that resulted in psychiatric disorders (Krafft-Ebing, R.V., 1965). Thirty years ago marked the beginning of regarding the psychopathology of sex offenses from the vantage point of rehabilitation. Since that time, to some extent, interest appears to have peaked and waned depending upon a number of variables, not the least of which have been public outrage and political expediency. In general, however, there has been a steady increase in the number of specialized programs to treat offenders based on the dual rationale of the need for scientific research and the concomitant need to decrease recidivism (Brecher, 1978).

In the early 1970's, we saw the emergence of a variety of innovative and eclectic approaches to treatment as analytic therapy was replaced by humanistic, behavioral and social learning models. Some of the new approaches were conventional: group confrontation, the incorporation of didactic material on sexual dysfunction, the use of female co-therapists, the participation of wives in therapy, and relationship counseling. Some others were more unconventional: the use of surrogate sex partners and pornography, the re-enactment of offenses on inflated dolls, or, with cases of exhibitionism, therapy in the presence of female therapists.[11]

Yet, by 1980, there were few definitive studies on sex offenders and still fewer that could withstand the careful scrutiny of data analysis. Many of the studies have been anecdotal, and while they provide valuable insights into the causes of sexually aggressive behavior, few provide useful information regarding therapeutic approaches that result in a measurable change in behavior over time. Even fewer of these studies contain quantitative data, with adequate samples, on success rates for controlling deviant behavior over time.

Brecher (1978) reports that currently no one can demonstrate that the twenty institutional and community-based programs surveyed in his report are more effective than imprisonment. He further states that one method of evaluating success appears to be "intuition." Glaser (1976) reports that the poor quality of evaluative research in criminal justice relates to the fact that program administrators have

---

[11]Some unconventional techniques, such as the use of surrogate sex partners, have been suggested but not put into practice for political and social reasons.

a vested interest in favorable results in order to meet eligibility requirements for public funding. One of Glaser's (1976) solutions to this dilemma is to assure outside monitoring for fiscal and quality control.

The notion that diagnosis precedes treatment is often not applied with sexually aggressive men. Even though there are recognizable differences among the types of sex offenders, similar treatment modalities are commonly recommended for all. In addition, there is, as yet, no adequate battery of assessment tools to detect high-risk offenders or to predict the likelihood of recidivist behavior. More effort is expended on refining therapeutic approaches than on formulating accurate diagnoses.

Major controversies still exist in the professional community regarding the characteristics and types of sex offenders. For example, incest offenders variously are described as introverted, aggressive, impulsive, overdependent with fears of abandonment, emotionally deprived and/or alcoholic (Watts and Courtois 1981). Justice and Justice (1979), on the other hand, identify four types of incest offenders: pedophilic, psychotic, psychopathic-promiscuous and symbioticalcoholic.

The current pre-eminence of the medical model (over the punitive) for management of sex offenders has serious implications for future trends in rehabilitation. Behavior that formerly was viewed as morally and legally wrong, i.e., harmful to self, others and society, now is labeled "sick." Conrad (1980) refers to the medicalization of deviance. The result is an abdication of individual responsibility for deviant behavior. The sex offender no longer is viewed as a criminal whose behavior is "sinful" or "bad" and who chooses to act in deviant ways that ultimately are under his control. Rather, he is seen as ill and in need of medical intervention. Behavior that can be explained as resulting from illness allows for rationalizations and the denial of free will (Livingston, 1974).

Acceptance of the medical model precludes or minimizes the importance of other interventions and approaches, such as the legal, and invests the medical professionals with inordinate power in an area in which they often possess little knowledge, background or expertise.   For example, the criminal justice system today almost routinely bestows upon physician-psychiatrists the title of "experts" and defers to their definitive pronouncements and predictions regarding etiology, diagnosis and prognosis for a sexually deviant criminal population that has barely begun to be examined in any depth.

Kovel (1980) refers to diagnosis as the Holy Grail of psychiatry and it does appear that the entire medical profession has almost been sanctified.   Ingleby (1980) notes that physician-psychiatrists in the U.S. write 200 million prescriptions for psychoactive drugs each year.   MacNamara reports that there is little empirical evidence to support the medical model.   Evaluative studies are fraught with errors; jail sentences are imposed with inconsistency; treatment is coerced; and recommended diversionary treatment programs often are not available.   In addition, use of the medical model inadvertently encourages power plays among professionals invested in maintaining status and enhancing their careers—probation and parole officers, therapists, lawyers, legislators and pressure groups.

The abandonment of the retributive-punitive model eliminates the deterrent impact of incarceration (MacNamara, 1978).   As Glaser (1976) notes, sexually aggressive men are more deterred by imprisonment than are most other types of criminals.

There is an additional problem that results from our reliance on the medical model which serves as an umbrella encompassing a wide array of specialists in behavioral health.   Often, these specialists are so totally oriented toward humanistic service that they neglect to consider the severity of the crimes with which they are dealing.   For example, sexual activity with children is classified as a crime in all fifty states and yet the literature on incest, for example, is concerned primarily with the social and familial aspects of the problem, rather than with the illegality of the behaviors (Pitcher, 1972; Adler, 1978; Broadhurst and Knoeller, 1979; Eskin, 1980; Zaphiris, 1980).

The jargon of the professional trade often further confounds clear issues such as guilt or innocence, as in Baily and Baily who refer to "human service analysts" (therapists?) who view sexual abuse as a "serious misalignment in family function" where offenders need to be available to help the family re-establish normal functioning. Baily and Baily (1983) even form an analogy between incest and mental retardation, citing the gradual social acceptance of the mentally retarded which has facilitated a helpful rather than a punitive approach to their problems. Brecher (1978) also refers to comparisons between sex offenders and the mentally retarded (as well as the poor, the exceptionally bright and the mentally ill). Sex offenders form a subgroup that, to some authorities, is entitled to the same social services as other social minorities.

At this point it should be noted that an "either-or" approach to sexually aggressive men is not being advocated but, rather, a cautious and ethical orientation to issues that affect the lives of victimized people of all ages. Statistics indicate that incarceration alone does not deter sex offenders from victimizing others (Abel, 1978). Of those individuals in prison for rape and then released, thirty-five to seventy percent will be returned to prison for the same crime (Watts and Courtois, 1981).

Yet, it appears as if a therapeutic response to incest and child molestation primarily serves as a rationale to protect male offenders under the guise of child-victim advocacy. Many therapeutic programs are designed to:

1) Protect victims and alleviate their guilt

2) Protect society from future prostitutes and chemical abusers by dealing with victims within the family context

3) Save society the cost and often fruitless efforts involved in prosecution

4) Free victims and passive mothers to resolve their problems while receiving financial support from offending spouses.

Often, however, the reality is that victims and others want offenders to be prosecuted to the full extent of the law and to be kept permanently off the streets and out of the home. Many victims seek validation and retribution for themselves, not rehabilitation for sex offenders.

What then, should be the role of the legal system? It appears that, at least, the criminal justice system should be improved to deal with the problems of cost-effectiveness and successful prosecution. Eliminating prosecution altogether (or softening the process via diversionary and plea bargaining programs), because it is currently costly and often ineffective, is a self-defeating solution to this serious legal issue. Victims and passive mothers do not necessarily become stronger and more assertive while still part of an enmeshed, interdependent triad that is supported emotionally and financially by an offending spouse.

Sex offenders have been segregated from the criminal population for rehabilitation at a time when professional therapists are novices, at best, in providing effective treatment, not to mention accurate diagnoses. The mistaken assumption of "treatability" has been based largely on a needed rationale to justify implementation of therapeutic programs.

Investing power in therapists (the medical and psychiatric community) has a broad range of anticipated and unanticipated effects. It results in a position of disinvolvement and deference to the medical establishment by the criminal justice system and the lay public. The dangers of this approach are obvious. Self-perpetuation can become the primary goal of behavioral health bureaucracies, often at the expense of fiscal and quality accountability to those whom they are designed to serve.

The trend toward selecting sex offenders for preferential treatment merits consideration. As a group, sex offenders have a history not dissimilar to that of other criminals. Generally, they also share many characteristics: low impulse control, expedient and ego-centric behavior, low frustration tolerance, a propensity toward chemical abuse, action orientation, manipulation, lack of empathy or objectification of others, and absence of both guilt and remorse for antisocial actions. Like the vast majority of our criminal population, sex offenders are emotionally disturbed men with histories of neglect and abuse.

Generally, character-disordered individuals commit antisocial acts; and crimes, whether premeditated or impulsive, clearly constitute antisocial acts. There is a recognized need to rehabilitate the prison population, for practical as well as humanitarian reasons, but clearly the approach has been essentially punitive and focused on incarceration as the most viable means to prevent recidivism.

Hence, it is interesting to examine reasons why time, energy and money are being invested in treating sexually aggressive males. One can only hypothesize on the rationale for a therapeutic orientation. Nonetheless, the issue merits attention in the event that biases may predominate which, in the long run, will affect objectivity. Certainly the acquisition of power, status and financial gain acts as a strong incentive among treatment providers. Among the other possible reasons for a treatment-orientation regarding sex offenders are:

1) **The persistence of minimization in regard to male crimes against the powerless.** In a society where women's equality remains an issue that continues to inspire debate, conflict and anger, there still may be an orientation toward acceptance of the male prerogative to possess and own his woman and children as property with which to do as he chooses.

2) **The need for titillation and vicarious enjoyment of deviant sexuality.** Television, motion pictures, journals, magazines and video films, in an effort to popularize and exploit sexuality, have helped to create a multi-million dollar industry with an audience of readers/viewers that receives vicarious gratification and titillation from indirect sexual experiences. Some of the articles and films receive legitimacy under the guise of being exposes, works of art or educational

endeavors. In parallel fashion, the field of sexuality attracts a number of emotionally unhealthy specialists who, under the guise of objectivity and professionalism, receive vicarious gratification from exposure to deviant behavior.

3) **An inability to tolerate the dissonance inherent in ambiguity.** The field of behavioral health involves human beings, and, by their very nature, human beings are complicated, variable and unpredictable. The criminal justice system, on the other hand, has developed a rigid set of rules and regulations which are arbitrarily applied to human behavior. Hence, an inherent conflict exists in the application of laws to behavior. That conflict is exacerbated when attempts are made to classify and categorize behavior to more perfectly fit existing laws. The conflict results in confusion and dissonance for which, inevitably, solutions are sought in order to maintain a comfort level. Simplistic solutions, predicated on rationalizations, resolve dissonance, at least temporarily.

4) **The presence of defensive reactions.** With the realization of each individual's sexuality and potential for deviant behavior, people react defensively when confronted with that potential fully actualized in the sexual offender. Among the more common defensive maneuvers employed are reaction formation (love turned to hate; hate turned to love), rationalization/minimization, and identification with the aggressor. An example of a defensive reaction can be seen in the therapist or attorney who unconsciously identifies with a sexually deviant client and becomes his advocate, usually as an impassioned, nonobjective and completely illogical champion of the offender's innocence.

On a practical level, it is easier to resolve the problem of deviant sexuality with the following rationale:

1) Human beings all are sexual with a (latent) potential for any kind of sexual behavior.

2) Since, theoretically, all individuals could be sexual deviants, people can minimize the threat and fear inherent in this realization by viewing the problem as a treatable illness.

3) Since the problem is a treatable illness, laws that do not accommodate variables, such as causation and motivation, do not apply to deviant sexuality.

In conclusion, it appears evident that the issues involved in planning for the protection of society from sexually aggressive men are complicated and merit serious and thoughtful attention. To seek simple solutions based on emotions rather than logic will result in the impulsive implementation of poorly tested innovative concept and techniques. Some of the very behaviors targeted to be curbed in the criminal population will be mimicked by society. If emotions predominate, there will be an exacerbation of inherent conflicts, antagonisms and polarizations among existing bureaucracies. Expert will be pitted against expert, female against male, and the criminal justice system against the therapeutic community.

In the meantime, sex offenders are on the streets. They fit into several categories: never apprehended, apprehended but never charged, charged but never convicted, on probation, incarcerated in jail while on work release/probation, and on parole subsequent to incarceration in prison.

In the absence of better solutions, therapy continues to be offered. What is desperately needed to help rehabilitative endeavors is objective research by impartial scientists; the disinvolvement of self-interest groups whose primary goals are self-perpetuation and the acquisition of power; extreme caution and cooperation among professionals, politicians, community members and the criminal justice system; the implementation of training programs in the departments of counseling, social work and psychology in our universities; and clear, logical thinking as the result of self-awareness among experts and authorities in the field.

Finally, nonoffending males must be encouraged to take a more active role in preventing offenses. In this regard, such community-based self-help programs as the Santa Cruz Men Against Rape program are helpful and effective ways for eliciting the maximum involvement of communities—men, women, and, professionals—in working together to ameliorate the problems of sexual offenses.

7

OFFENDERS IN TREATMENT:
A Profile

A descriptive profile detailing the characteristics of a sample of incestuous offenders in therapy can yield a wealth of useful information. Such a profile is essential for therapists interested in careful assessment and an accurate prognosis. The data presented here are taken from a two-year study of thirty-nine incest offenders, twenty-seven of whom were seen in long-term group and individual therapy on an outpatient basis. The remaining twelve were seen on a short-term basis for assessment prior to court action. All of the men were referred by adult probation, child protective services, and therapists in agency and private practice. Several of the offenders had not yet completed therapy at the time of this study.

Review of these data is important for therapists. In the presence of often disarming, repentant offenders who appear highly motivated to receive therapy prior to conviction and sentencing, therapists often forget that their client population is largely diagnosed as character-disordered, and is, therefore, highly manipulative and untrustworthy.

Readers may be surprised at some of the data presented—data that reveals recidivism, multiple assaults on several children in the family, high rates of genital and attempted genital intercourse, and the early age of the child victims at the onset of abuse.

Unfortunately, some of the data are valid only to the degree that self-reporting is an accurate measure of behavior. In addition, observational research has advantages and drawbacks. Among the disadvantages is the influence of the observers/therapists on the data, i.e., their biases and perceptual shortcomings. On the positive side, long-term observation maximizes the influence of observers who can evaluate and reformulate their perceptions, and have the opportunity to experience the process of change and conflict resolution of the clients (Livingston, 1974).

In this sample, the clients were not imprisoned. Hence, unlike incarcerated offenders who self-disclose, the men did not fear retaliation from fellow inmates. On the other hand, some of the offenders were guarded because they were anticipating involvement in court proceedings.

Some of the information reported is clearly factual, i.e., identifying information, socio-economic data, prior misdemeanors and felonies, and current charges. Part of the information is incomplete. For example, as a defense, adult victims of sexual or physical abuse sometimes partially or completely block early trauma. Hence, they are capable of disclosing only partial childhood histories. In addition, subjectivity affects accuracy. More than one offender did not perceive his childhood as physically or sexually abusive, even though, both legally and ethically, he was a victim of child abuse.

On the positive side, most of the men experienced a high trust level in therapy resulting in honesty and open self-disclosures. Many were seen in therapy for two years in different contexts and under varying degrees of stress. Finally, corroborative data was obtained from a variety of sources including child protective services, the courts, police, probation officers and family members.

Twelve of the thirty-nine offenders profiled were evaluated as poor candidates for therapy due to a variety of factors including the degree of psychopathology, history of recidivism and/or prior sex crimes, presence of fixed pedophilic behavior, chronic substance abuse, and low mental functioning. The variable common to all twelve of the untreatable offenders, however, was the presence of persistent denial following disclosure. The impasse of denial was not broken even following initial therapeutic interventions.

Identifying Information

Ages When Entering Treatment	Number	Percentage
24-30	4	10%
31-40	29	75
41-50	4	10
51-60	2	5

Comments: The data concerning the ages of offenders in treatment are consistent with that in the literature on incest where the average offender is in his mid-thirties at the time of disclosure. The two offenders over the age of fifty were both grandfathers who molested (fondled) their seven- and three-year-old granddaughters, respectively. One of the grandfathers had molested his daughters thirty years prior to the current offense.

Years Married	Number	Percentage
Less than 10 years	6	16%
10-14 years	16	41
15-20 years	14	36
20+ years	3	7
Prior Marriages		
0	32	82
1	7	18

Comments: For eight of the offenders, divorce followed disclosure of incest.   While only seven of the offenders had an earlier history of divorce, twelve of the wives had had prior marriages.   Four of these wives were considerably older than their spouses.   Incestuous families generally are intact with long-term marriages.

Ethnic Background	Number	Percentage
Caucasian	34	87%
Black	2	5
Mexican American	2	5
Other	1	3

Comments: This study was conducted in a metropolitan area of the southwest.   Hence, generalizations from the data are limited; and, ethnic, religious and other identifying information cannot be considered to be representative of the larger population.

Religion	Number	Percentage
Catholic	15	38%
Baptist	10	26
Presbyterian	8	21
Mormon (LDS)	3	8
Jehovah's Witnesses	2	5
Pentecostal	1	2

Comments: Upon disclosure of their incestuous behavior in the home, three formerly nonreligious offenders became born-again Christians. Turning to religion in times of extreme stress is not atypical behavior for sex offenders, and appears to be a manifestation of projecting responsibility onto a higher power.

Level of Education (Years Completed)	Number	Percentage
Elementary school	3	8%
Some high school or GED (General Equivalency Diploma)	6	15
High school diploma; Some college or AA degree (Associate of	21	54
Arts, two-year degree)	8	21
BA or BS degree	1	2

Occupation	Number	Percentage
Labor (sanitation worker, ditch digger, dishwasher)	13	33%
Blue collar (cook, mechanic, truck driver)	11	28
White collar (engineer, policeman, technician, teacher, salesman)	13	33
Professional (investor, manager)	2	6

Comments: There was considerable variation in employment stability among the offenders. However, fourteen of the laborers and blue collar workers had sporadic job histories with several job changes per year, along with frequent moves in and out of state. One offender changed jobs thirty times in ten years. Several of the men serving jail/work release advanced vocationally while incarcerated. They worked long hours, possibly to avoid painful rumination and additional hours in jail, rather than to enhance their vocational status. Even though many of the families were under considerable financial stress, seventeen of the wives were unemployed. Of those who were working, thirteen held blue collar positions; five, white collar; and four, labor.   The fact that thirty-nine percent of the women were unemployed when their families were experiencing economic hardship lends credence to the notion that mothers of incest victims tend to be dependent and socially isolated.

Geographic Region of Origin	Number	Percentage
Midwest	17	43%
South	8	21
Southwest	8	21
West	2	5
East	2	5
Northwest	2	5

Comments: Southern Illinois, Missouri (Ozarks), Kansas, Oklahoma, Kentucky, Texas and Arizona were heavily represented in this sample derived from a southwestern city.

Abuse in Childhood	Number	Percentage
Physically abused	18	46%
Physically and sexually abused	9	23
Sexually abused	20	51
Single perpetrator	15	38
Multiple molestation	5	13
Perpetrator father	1	3
Perpetrator mother	5	13
Perpetrator sister	2	5
Perpetrator male, nonrelative	9	23
Perpetrator female, nonrelative	3	8

Comments: It is possible that sexual abuse in the backgrounds of the offenders was more prevalent than the data reveals. Several of the men did not remember being victimized until they had been group participants for six months or longer. Often, recall of a traumatic event was triggered suddenly in the group setting. In addition, some of the men were reluctant to disclose abuse by a mother or older male due to shame and embarrassment. With regard to the categories, "male, nonrelative," and "female, nonrelative," many of the perpetrators were older baby-sitters or caretakers. In seven of the families, both offender and spouse had experienced molestation as children. Seventeen of the wives of the offenders had also been sexually abused in childhood.

Subjective factors marred the data regarding physical abuse. A number of the offenders rationalized the severity of abuse perpetrated against them and argued in favor of corporal punishment. Many of the men were steadfast in their refusal to characterize as abusive the punishment they received in childhood. At the same time, they described early childhood experiences fraught with sadistic abuse:

"My mother had me kneel on corn kernels all night long."

"I still have hose marks on my back from where my father beat me."

"My mother stamped on my foot when it was in a cast."

"My legs looked so bad that I would never wear shorts."

"One time, my brother threw a shovel at me and I ducked and it hit my mother. She was so mad that she beat me up—not my brother."

Anger, consciously or unconsciously experienced, resulted from the abusive backgrounds of the men. Hackett (1971) reports that anger was present in each of the thirty-seven court-referred offenders whom he treated.

Chemical Abuse	Number	Percentage
Alcohol only	16	41%
Drugs only	1	3
Polysubstances	6	15

Comments: Chemical abuse was a life-long chronic problem for the offenders. Many of them began abusing chemicals in their teen years or earlier. Chemical use was directly associated with incestuous behavior as a contributive but not causative factor. The wives of the offenders were relatively free of chemical abuse with two women claiming alcohol abuse, and two others claiming polysubstance abuse.

Associated Problems	Number	Percentage
Drug pushers	5	13%
Prior convictions (grand larceny, aggravated assault)	2	5
Prior sex-related crimes	14	36
Homicide/suicide	1	3
Recent hospitalizations (reactive depression, dissociative reaction, schizophrenic reaction)	7	18
Psychogenic problems (chronic back pain, migraines, ulcers)	14	36
Suicidal ideation— chronic, stress-related	18	46
Violent behavior (including battering)	15	38

Comments: Many of the offenders were suffering from borderline personality disorders and had experienced serious problems since childhood. Their early lives were characterized by rejection, abuse, neglect, violence and social isolation. Many had experienced a number of adjustment problems in school, including truancy, running away and fighting—all possible predictors of future antisocial, acting-out behaviors.

All of the offenders had problems controlling impulses, especially anger, in varying degrees. One broke a tennis racket with his bare hands, while in a rage over some petty incident; several had punched in walls; and at least half had struck their spouses at least once. Some of the men openly expressed their anger; others remained inhibited, repressed and fearful of their impulses; and the remainder tended to behave passive-aggressively.

Angry impulses were often directed inward in the form of suicidal thoughts and aborted suicide attempts. As stress mounted, self-esteem diminished and suicide became a viable alternative to coping. Many of the men had experienced suicidal thoughts at the time of disclosure. Some of them deliberately avoided situations that might trigger suicidal impulses, such as driving, keeping weapons at home, or mountain climbing. One man shot his wife, attempted to shoot his children, and killed himself shortly after incest with his thirteen-year-old daughter was disclosed.

Anger and violence were linked to sexual aggression. A number of the men characterized seduction as, "the four F's," i.e., "find 'em, feel 'em, fuck 'em and forget 'em." While their wives generally were conservative and sexually inhibited, the men enjoyed a variety of sexual practices ranging from extensive use of pornography and group sex to such clearly defined perversions as urologia. Sexual incompatibility with their wives was a major concern for the offenders, especially in those marriages where the women had unresolved feelings related to their own molestations.

Eleven of the men had histories of reported and unreported sex crimes. Six men were recidivist incest offenders. Only two of the earlier offenses had been reported to the authorities. Five men had been exhibitionists: one had been charged with four separate counts of indecent exposure ten and seven years prior to disclosure of incest with his daughter; a second man had exhibited himself before his mother-in-law, and had attempted molestation of his twenty-three-year-old sister-in-law when she was thirteen. (Neither incident had been reported to the police or child protective services.)

Two of the offenders had lengthy histories of sexual offenses. At the time that incest was disclosed, one of the men was also charged with child molestation involving forty-eight children. Five years prior to the current allegation of long-term incest with his eleven-year-old daughter, a second offender had avoided detection for such offenses as gang rape and compulsive voyeurism.

One of the grandfathers profiled had molested both of his natural daughters when they were children. Disclosure occurred a full thirty years after the cessation of abuse. One of the offenders, previously charged with sexual assault of a minor child, had plea bargained to aggravated assault and served a probationary sentence ten years prior to the current charge.

Seven of the men had been in psychiatric wards. One had experienced dissociative reactions during periods of stress; three had had schizophrenic episodes involving hallucinations, delusions of grandeur and violent behavior; and three had experienced reactive depressions following disclosure of incest.

Information regarding prior undisclosed sex offenses is particularly important in assessing the treatability of perpetrators. In addition, precipitous decisions regarding so-called nonviolent offenders must be avoided. For example, by whose criteria has it been determined that exhibitionists, voyeurs and child molesters constitute a nonviolent group? The measure of violence is not predicated solely on the infliction of physical harm. Even if exhibitionism/voyeurism does belong on the lower end of the continuum of violence, there is no guarantee that the perpetrator will continue to operate at that level. A proclivity toward nonviolence at one time does not mean that progressive deterioration will not result in future violent acting out. Finally, it cannot be said with certainty that the so-called passive offender has not acted out violently in the past.

Molestation–Types of Victims	Number	Percentage
Natural daughter	19	47%
Natural son	1	3
Stepdaughter	10	26
Adopted daughter	3	8
Girlfriend's daughter (live-in)	3	8
Granddaughter	2	5
Other (niece, minor, sister-in-law, etc.)	1	3

Comments: The figures above reflect current charges/allegations at the time of this study. One of the offenders, a fixated pedophile, had molested forty-eight children in addition to his daughter. Thirteen of the men either were recidivist offenders with the same child or had molested/attempted to molest other children in their families.

Age (Years) of Victim at Time of Disclosure	Number	Percentage
3-5 years	4	10%
6-10 years	4	10
11-13 years	14	36
14-16 years	17	44

Comments: One of the offenders was not reported until his daughter was twenty years old. Children in the three-to-five-year old age bracket sometimes did not directly disclose incest. The presence of molestation was determined through a variety of assessment tools revealing a cluster of symptoms indicative of molestation, i.e., the Child Sexual Abuse Syndrome, drawings that were sexually explicit, re-enactment of sexual acts with anatomically-correct dolls, behavioral changes, compulsive masturbation, insertion (by the victim) of objects into the vagina, fear of perpetrators, nightmares, psychosomatic complaints, sudden onset of fears and regressed behavior.

Nature of Abuse	Number	Percentage (rounded)
Fondling/digital penetration, masturbation	13	33%
Exhibitionism/voyeurism	2	5
Genital/anal intercourse	11	28
Attempted/completed Intercourse	13	33

Comments: Molestation of the four children in the three- to five-year-old age bracket involved fondling and masturbation. One pregnancy and one feared pregnancy resulted from sexual intercourse involving natural daughters. Intercourse with the victims usually was painful, i.e., rape. Generally, the younger the victim, the more she had to endure polymorphous perversion. Offenders of preschool children often manifest a variety of bizarre, sometimes sadistic, acting-out behaviors. These behaviors often involve rituals associated with urination and defecation.

Circumstances of Disclosure	Number	Percentage
Victim self-disclosed to non-family member	31	79%
Victim self-disclosed to mother	4	10
Offender confessed	2	5
Offender caught during molestation	2	5

Comments: Of the thirty-one girls who disclosed to non-family members, the vast majority told an adult at school or a close friend, who then reported the abuse to an adult. Of the four victims who disclosed molestation to their mothers, three were under five and their disclosures were vague, inconsistent and/or indirect. A therapist had to complete a full assessment to determine the identity of the perpetrator and the nature of the molestation. The fact that most of the victims did not disclose incest to a family member lends credence to the notion that incestuous families are enmeshed and nonprotective of the victim.

Reaction of Offenders at Time of Disclosure	Number	Percentage
Denial (initial)	37	92%
Denial (continuing)	12	31
Rationalization/ minimization (subsequent to denial)	15	38
Confession (initial)	2	4

Comments: The vast majority of sexual offenders initially deny their behavior. Fear of reprisals and the inability to accept responsibility and/or ego-dystonic behavior appear to be prime motivations for denial. For many offenders, minimization and rationalization follow denial and can persist in varying degrees throughout the therapeutic process. Minimization and rationalization take many forms, some more detrimental to the therapeutic process than others. For example, it was only after six to nine months in group therapy that a number of the men admitted that they had always fantasized about sex with young children.

The offender who persists in minimizing the extent of sexual abuse, who claims that there was no sexual intent behind his behavior, and/or who insists that the child victims provoked him into molesting them, clearly is character-disordered and is not a good candidate for therapy. If, on the other hand, denial appears to be a defense against experiencing guilt or anxiety, the prognosis may be more favorable.

Generally, offenders confess only to acts that their victims allege, or to fewer acts than alleged. If their victims do not disclose, the offenders do not confess, and, in the case of preschool children, they deny their behaviors with the full knowledge that abuse cannot be proven in court. Perpetrators of incestuous abuse rarely disclose all of their behaviors, particularly the devious, coercive and manipulative acts associated with the molestation. None of the men in the sample indicated that they had taken nude photographs of their victims or shown them kiddie porn, and yet, in therapy, many of the girls alleged that these acts had, indeed, occurred. Finally, all of the men except the few who confessed eventually admitted that incestuous abuse would have continued had not their daughters and stepdaughters self-disclosed.

Age (Years) of Victim at Onset of Abuse	Number	Percentage
0-5	8	21%
6-11	27	69
12-14	4	10

Comments: Data on a national level also indicate that the average age of onset of sexual abuse is six to eleven years of age. However, perpetrators with preschool victims rarely admit their offenses because there can be no legally valid corroboration from the children as witnesses. Victims who disclose in their teen or pre-teen years often do not recall their ages at the onset of abuse.

Professionals working in the field of child sexual abuse suspect that a larger proportion of preschool children are sexually victimized than is commonly known, and that often, for long-term molestation, the age of onset is under five.

Among the children under six in this sample, six were three and four years of age at the time of this study. Hence, there are no follow-up data regarding their emotional and behavioral status. Between the remaining two, the combination of long-term molestation (six and ten years, respectively), early age at the onset of abuse and the nature of the molestation, all contributed to severe emotional and behavioral difficulties for the girls, i.e., hospitalization for psychiatric problems and therapeutic foster home care. One of the girls began to molest other children before she reached the age of thirteen.

Length of Time (Years) of Sexual Abuse	Number	Percentage
0-2 years	7	18%
3-5 years	27	69
6-10 years	5	13

Comments: The data pertains to allegations current at the time when the men were in therapy. Over the years, eight of the offenders had molested several of their children. This information was not known to the courts at the time of sentencing. In addition, a number of the men initially had approached one child and, following rejection, proceeded to molest another one of their offspring.

Disposition for Child Following Disclosure	Number	Percentage
Short-term shelter or foster care	3	8%
Long-term foster care or psychiatric hospitalization	4	10
Remained in home; offender left (temporarily or permanently)	32	82

Comments: Children were removed from the home following child protective services assessment that their mothers would not protect them from further abuse. In three instances, both children and offenders left the home. In one of these cases involving incestuous abuse of ten years duration, the mother beat her fifteen-year-old daughter with a board when the girl disclosed incest. In a second instance, where pregnancy resulted from the molestation, the mother, also pregnant by the same man, totally rejected her daughter and openly blamed her for provocative behavior. Some of the girls did not adjust to shelter or foster care and experienced multiple placements in less than six months following disclosure.

The statistics reflect an optimistic picture in that eighty-two percent of the victims were able to remain in their own home. In reality, many of the victims suffered dire consequences following disclosure. Their mothers and siblings, experiencing problems of their own, tended to blame the victims for family disruption. It was common for mothers to use coercive and manipulative measures to convince victims to tell authorities that they wanted their fathers/stepfathers returned to the home.

Legal Consequences to the Offender.[12]

	Number	Percentage (rounded)
No legal consequence	14	36%
Long-term probation	8	21
Pending at time of study	7	18
Jail (30 days) with work release	4	11
Jail (up to one year), work release, and probation	4	11
Prison (longer than one year)	1	3

---

[12]One of the offenders committed suicide.

Comments: All thirty-nine cases were reported to both child protective services and the police. In some instances, the police did not follow through with an investigation if the abuse occurred prior to the expiration of the statute of limitations, or if the child was under five years of age and considered incompetent to testify in court. In one case, child protective services sent the child to another state to live with her natural mother and there was no follow-up either by the child protective services or the police (even though the victim returned to her father's care within six months of her departure). In another case, motile sperm were found during a medical examination of the child following disclosure. Since the girl's father had had a vasectomy, there was no follow-up by the police.[13]

Discussion:

In spite of the fact that the data from this study of sex offenders were collected from a particular region of the United States, i.e., a region attracting transients, midwesterners and certain religious groups, the men profiled in this sample appear to be fairly representative of incest offenders seeking outpatient therapy either by choice or coercion. Such men rarely are screened thoroughly (if at all) prior to referral for therapy, and they present a wide range of symptomatology. Becoming aware of symptoms enables therapists to form prognoses and to distinguish among possibly treatable and untreatable offenders.

From the data, it appears that at the time of disclosure, the average incest offender is a male in his thirties, employed in a wide range of occupations, and married for a number of years. He

---

[13]Two years after the alleged abuse had ceased, a dedicated prosecutor followed up on this complicated case. The victim, then psychotic and in a state hospital, was not a very credible witness. Nonetheless, through this prosecutor's thorough investigation and use of numerous expert witnesses, the offending father was found guilty on four counts of child molestation and sentenced to over thirty years imprisonment.

may well have an unstable employment history and probably has been experiencing various degrees of interpersonal, financial, vocational and social stresses for some time.   He tends to be isolated with a limited social, emotional and behavioral repertoire. Lack of communication and sexual problems have characterized his marriage, and he might have married a woman who was sexually abused as a child and who has her own problems related to unresolved trauma.

The typical incest offender experienced behavioral and emotional problems during childhood where sexual and/or physical abuse were commonplace.   As a result, he is angry and sometimes violent.   Anger is often turned inward, expressing itself in depression or suicidal thoughts.   His self-image is poor and he is unaware of underlying feelings of inadequacy and rage.   Stress, often the catalyst for the onset of incestuous behavior, compounds feelings of anger and impotence.

Fifty-nine percent of the offenders sampled had histories of chemical abuse along with a number of other serious problems, including prior sex offenses and psychogenic difficulties.   Denial, as a defense, and depression, as an emotional reaction, characteristically are associated with the disclosure of incest in the home.

Sexual problems, ignorance regarding sexuality, male-female sex-role stereotyping, and difficulties with emotional intimacy all are commonplace among incest offenders.   Partly due to childhood associations, sex is associated with anger and violence.   Incest often appears to serve as an indirect, passive-aggressive release for displaced anger of early, unmet needs for nurturing as well as for subsequent feelings of rejection.

It seems clear that there really is no obvious or definitive profile of an incest offender.   A number of the superficial attributes of such men are typical of many individuals.   However, descriptively, incest offenders do tend to have high rates of chemical abuse, histories of physical and/or sexual abuse in their backgrounds (with resultant anger, sexual and communication problems, and poor interpersonal and vocational skills).

Daughters and stepdaughters typically are the victims of incestuous abuse which usually begins between the ages of six and eleven, lasts three to five years, and is not disclosed until the victim reaches puberty or pre-puberty. Attempted genital/anal intercourse is a common form of abuse, as is dry intercourse and actual penetration. Recidivism is not uncommon. Lack of trust permeates the incestuous family, and it is not common for child victims to disclose abuse first to their mothers. Usually a nonrelative is the first person to be informed that molestation has been occurring in the family. Instead of receiving sympathy and support, victims generally are punished by their families and treated poorly by the court system, for disclosing sexual abuse.[14]

All too often, there are no serious legal consequences for incestuous abusers. Of the thirty-nine offenders sampled, only one went to prison. Children remained at home or were removed for a short period of time to allow the authorities to complete their investigations.

Some of the results of this study simply corroborate data that the authorities in the field believe characterize the incestuous family. Several points, however, merit emphasis. Of the twelve men assessed as poor candidates for therapy, eight had persisted in denying sexual

---

[14]At the end of this study, seventeen of the daughter/stepdaughter victims were teenagers between the ages of thirteen and eighteen. Each had been involved the various therapy programs for a year or longer. It is significant that not one of the teenage victims wanted her father/stepfather returned to the home. None of the girls wanted their mothers to know her feelings. The basic message each girl gave was, "He counts more than I do," and, "If I tell my mother how I feel, the family will fall apart—I'll get blamed." About their fathers/stepfathers the girls said, "He hasn't changed; he's still a pervert; I don't feel comfortable around him." On the positive side, the girls generally believed re-molestation would not occur because they would prevent it by disclosing either to their therapists or the police.

abuse and/or were involved in criminal court cases where their daughters were forced to testify against them in open court. Four of the untreatable men had severe emotional problems prior to sex crimes, and limited intellectual functioning/capacity for insight. These four key factors—persistent denial, severe psychopathology, limited intelligence and a prior history of sex crimes—were of paramount importance in formulating negative prognoses. Few of the thirty-nine men had very favorable prognoses. Long-term monitoring and support were deemed essential to safeguard children. Prognoses for the children varied and were contingent upon improved motherdaughter bonding. Unfortunately, in many of the cases, bonding between mothers and child victims was irrevocably impaired.

8

APPROACHES TO TREATMENT

Case managers, probation and parole officers, as well as therapists, should become familiar with the specific treatment approaches currently in use with sexually aggressive men. Traditionally, psychotherapy has been the most commonly used treatment modality with all clinical populations. Authorities now are aware of the limitations of one-on-one "talk therapy" for obsessive, antisocial criminal sex offenders (Watts, 1981). Sexually aggressive males often lack feelings of guilt or remorse, i.e., the neurotic suffering that motivates people to change dysfunctional behavioral patterns. In addition, this population sometimes lacks the capacity to absorb and assimilate the insights that precede constructive behavioral change. In general, one-on-one primary psychotherapeutic approaches have been supplemented or replaced by behavioral, medical, humanistic and social learning models; also, clients are seen individually, as well as in group, family, milieu, marital, psychodrama and self-help therapy.

The treatment choice for sex offenders ideally should depend upon a number of variables including diagnoses, prognoses, overall treatment plans, case management, and the feasibility of implementation and monitoring. Unless treatment methods clearly are designated as experimental, they should be based on success rates derived from research studies.   In addition, especially when dealing with the criminal population, treatment providers should be specialists with experience and expertise in working with sexual aggressive.   More often than not, the above-listed guidelines are not followed.

Behavioral Therapy

In work with sex offenders, behavioral management therapy now outnumbers other available modalities two to one (Langevin, 1983). Behavioral therapy is definitive and time-limited with the possibility of at least short-term measurement of change.   Although use of the various methods requires some degree of skill, they are relatively easy and quick to learn and require little from therapists, other than technical training.

A wide variety of behavioral techniques is in use today in controlled settings, such as institutions and prisons, as well as in outpatient clinics and agencies.   Use appears to be somewhat random, without consideration of history or severity of offenses.

For example, a chronic, fixated pedophile may well receive the same treatment as a violent rapist or regressed incest offender.   All of the techniques are based on learning theory which holds that behavior is learned and, therefore, can be unlearned.   The aim is to reduce deviant arousal responses and to increase socially acceptable ones.

Aversion therapy, a form of behavior management, is detailed in much of the existing literature (Knopp, F. H., 1984; Langevin, R., 1983; Brecher, E. M., 1978, and others).   Basically it involves the administration of a shock (electrical) or noxious chemical when the offender experiences erotic responses to an inappropriate stimulus such as the photograph of a young child.   In other words, the conditioned response (public masturbation, for example) is paired with an aversive stimulus (electric shock) with the expectation of extinguishing the deviant behavior.

Olfactory aversion works quickly and is used by some therapists who are preparing to meet a court deadline in which they to attest to the treatability of their clients. Offenders are given crushable vials or perfume bottles filled with ammonia to carry with them outside of the laboratory setting, with the expectation that they will self-administer the aversive odor when they experience an impulse to molest or flash.

Covert sensitization, one of the many variations of aversion therapy, involves instructing the offender to fantasize the deviant behavior with negative results. For example, an incest offender might imagine a scenario in which he enters his daughter's bedroom and begins to fondle her when his wife opens the door and shoots him.

Boredom aversion (Laws and O'Neil, 1979; Marshall and Lippens, 1977), involves instructing the offender to masturbate to orgasm to a socially appropriate fantasy. He then spends forty-five minutes to one hour recording deviant fantasies.

The Modified Aversive Behavioral Technique (MABT), used by the Northwest Treatment Associates in Seattle, Washington, requires offenders to re-enact sexual assault on mannequins. Sessions are videotaped and replayed, sometimes in group settings, to shame the patient and highlight the absurdity and destructiveness of his behavior.

In addition to aversive techniques, behavior therapy offers a number of simple impulse control techniques, such as thought stopping, thought shifting, and impulse charting. In thought stopping, the offender is instructed to silently repeat a phrase or word such as, "Stop!" as he starts to have deviant thoughts or to experience unacceptable impulses. Thought shifting requires him to substitute a negative image, such as being arrested by the police, at the moment of arousal. Impulse charting is a method of control involving the recording of the number and intensities of deviant impulses. The act of recording itself becomes aversive, and thereby decreases the frequency of deviant impulses.

Systematic desensitization or reciprocal inhibition is based on the principle that an individual cannot experience two competing responses simultaneously. For example, one cannot experience tension if one's body is relaxed. The offender first is instructed in techniques of deep muscle relaxation developed by Jacobsen. While in a relaxed state, he then is presented with a hierarchy of anxiety-producing events, from weakest to strongest, in order to increase desired responses. The process is slow, and an offender is instructed to indicate (by raising his hand, for example) anxiety experienced at any level on the hierarchy. If, for example, the patient feels anxious at level three on the hierarchy, he so indicates, and the instructor begins the process again, starting at the first level.

Systematic desensitization has been used with homosexuals desiring to increase heterosexual responses. An illustrative hierarchy might begin with seeing an attractive woman (level one) to introducing oneself (level four) to requesting a date (level twelve).

Orgasmic reconditioning or masturbatory reconditioning (Abel and Blanchard, 1974; Marquis, 1970), involves instructing the offender to fantasize a deviant scenario to the point of orgasm, but change the fantasy to a socially acceptable one at the moment of ejaculation. The process involves shaping, i.e., the gradual approximation of socially acceptable fantasies, and usually is practiced twice weekly in a laboratory setting. Orgasmic reconditioning actually violates principles of behavior modification by pairing equally to a deviant and nondeviant stimulus. Hence, its use is not founded on a sound theoretical base.

Assertiveness training is a form of behavioral therapy. Clients are educated regarding three styles of communication, i.e., passive, assertive and aggressive. Assertive responses are practiced in sessions, and homework, via contracting for change, is assigned. Assertiveness therapy involves use of audio and videotaping for feedback, self-rewards for reinforcement, and coaching and modeling by therapists. It has been used with pedophiles who have difficulties socializing with peers of either sex, with violent offenders who lack control of their anger, and with incest offenders who express anger through passive-aggressive behaviors.

There are a number of other behavioral methods, but most of them are variations of the ones presented above. In order to use some of these techniques, the behaviorist needs a "laboratory" e-quipped with various devices to measure responses: recording and videotaping systems, timers, shock boxes, feedback switches, penis circumference strain gauges, penile phallometers (used to measure penile volume during arousal) and others.

Langevin (1984) lists the numerous problems associated with be-havioral therapy. As with other treatment strategies for sex of-fenders, research studies on effectiveness have been limited. Op-ponents of behaviorism stress the need to focus on underlying causa-tive issues. Symptom shift or substitution may occur if deep-seated conflicts are not resolved. Some opponents also believe that behavior-al therapy is effective with specific symptoms such as stuttering, enuresis, and phobias, but not with complex maladaptive patterns seen in sexually aggressive men.

Many of the techniques currently in use violate principles of behavioral theory and, therefore, there is no logical or theoretical basis for their application. In addition, practitioners ignore the methodological principles of validity and reliability. Less than five percent of studies used a control group, baseline and adequate fol-low-up (McNamara and Macdonough, 1972).

Langevin expresses concern that behaviorists often make no dis-tinction between the concepts of suppression and extinction. In oth-er words, following behavioral therapy, symptoms may be in temporary abeyance and subject to recurrence, rather than permanently elimin-ated.

An additional concern expressed by a number of authorities re-lates to the principle of generalization and how that principle operates in practice rather than in theory. Ideally, responses learned in therapy should generalize to the external environment. In reality, however, this principle does not always apply.

For example, a pedophile in therapy receives electric shocks each time he is aroused by a series of photographs of young boys. He may learn to respond aversively to those particular youngsters, but not to other male children he sees in the outside world. Overgeneralization may occur as well. After undergoing aversion therapy, a pedophile might respond negatively not only to pubescent girls, but to all females.

Hence, there are a number of problems associated with behavioral therapy, not the least of which is the ethics involved in using painful laboratory tools and manipulative techniques with human beings. Refinements in procedures clearly are needed as well as data-based, methodologically sound research studies on the short- and long-term effectiveness of behavioral modification techniques.

Measures of Erectile Response[15]

A behavioral treatment and assessment approach meriting separate attention due to its increased use involves devices (penile phallometers and strain gauges) designed to measure volumetric or circumferential penile tumescence. Sexual arousal to appropriate or inappropriate stimuli is measured by increases in penile tumescence. Various behavioral methods such as aversion therapy then are used to condition appropriate responses.

Part of the rationale underlying the use of devices to measure penile response relates to the inadequacy of other assessment methods needed to formulate treatment strategies. For example, self-report

---

[15]For a complete description of the behavioral laboratory and its inventory, refer to: Greer, J. G. and Stuart, I. R. *The Sexual Aggressor: Current Perspectives on Treatment.* New York: Van Nostrand Reinhold Company, 1983.

by the offender and clinical judgment by the therapist are not accurate measures of arousal states.

Hypnosis, Guided Imagery, and Visualization.

Hypnosis, imagery and fantasy work have been used with sexually aggressive men. Under hypnosis, the offender fantasizes a deviant situation and experiences a negative result. He then fantasizes a socially appropriate situation and is rewarded with a positive outcome. Guided imagery and visualization are used similarly, or as tension reducing strategies. Both techniques are used to help alter destructive behaviors. Conditioned responses are altered with conscious suggestions or mental images of healthy change. For sex offenders, these techniques might involve a fantasy journey or visualization of a desired behavior, such as a mutually satisfying heterosexual relationship.

Biofeedback

Biofeedback trains the patient to measure stress levels by monitoring physiological reactions such as heart rate, skin temperature and galvanic changes. While not a primary therapy, biofeedback, nonetheless, has adjunctive value for stress reduction for sex offenders.

Surgical Castration

Surgical castration, included here because it is a feasible alternative for sex offenders, is not strictly a treatment modality. Physical incapacitation is not used in the United States at this time. Castration involves the surgical excision of the testicles. The testicles produce male sexual hormones. Excision prevents the production of semen, but does not alter the capacity to attain an erection.

Moreover, anger is recognized as a major factor in many sexual assaults. Therefore, it is hypothesized that castration could exacerbate the rage in offenders and, thus, increase the number of sexual assaults that are perpetrated. Available data may contradict this hypothesis. Sturup (1960) conducted a twenty-year Danish study of sex offenders by comparing various treatment methods. Offenders treated with hormones and therapy had a recidivism rate of 29.6 percent for sex crimes. Castrated offenders, on the other hand, had a recidivism of 3.5 percent for sex crimes. Castrated offenders also had lower recidivism rates for nonsexual crimes (Sturup, 1960).

Chemical Castration

Antihormone therapy for sex offenders, currently in use in Maryland, Illinois, Oregon, California and at the University of Texas at Galveston, has been implemented for some time. A number of authorities believe that voluntary chemical castration will be the preferred treatment modality of the future; others are more cautious regarding widespread implementation of drug programs as a reversible method of controlling sexual behavior. Hence, the use of antiandrogens, injected intramuscularly, is currently controversial.

Androgen is responsible for male development, while its absence leads to feminization. It is the "libido" hormone that accounts for sexual arousal in both sexes.

Depo Provera

A testosterone-suppressing drug, medroxyprogesterone acetate, marketed as Depo Provera, was originally developed as a female contraceptive. It has been linked to the growth of cancer in female laboratory animals and has been used at Johns Hopkins Hospital since 1966 to decrease sexual urges in offenders. F.D.A. approval has been pending since January, 1983, although the hormone has been approved by the World Health Organization and is used by more than eighty countries as a contraceptive (Newman, 1984). Several authorities in the field report that the use of Depo Provera decreases libido, i.e., erotic fantasies preceding acting-out behaviors, erections and ejaculations (Bradford, 1983; Berlin & Meinecke, 1981).

The drug is a recommended treatment for offenders who pose a threat to the community as well as for exhibitionists who are bombarded with uncontrolled sexual urges. It appears to give relief from intense sexual impulses, and the effects are reversible. Moreover, it may be the only viable treatment method for severely mentally handicapped and chronically mentally ill sexual offenders.

Depo Provera is administered to the patient following a baseline measurement of the testosterone level. Thereafter, the drug usually is administered intramuscularly every seven to ten days until the testosterone level is suppressed. The method of administering Depo Provera thus poses certain financial and logistical problems for users.

Despite apparently successful results with Depo Provera, its effectiveness appears to be limited and inconclusive (Langevin, 1983; Sun, 1984). Among the specific problems associated with use are the following:

1) Side effects are numerous and include weight gain, headaches, lethargy, sweats, nightmares, dyspnea, hyperglycemia, hypogonadism, leg cramps, thrombotic disorders, depression, fluid retention, infertility, liver damage and diabetes (Langevin, 1983).

2) The underlying assumption justifying use of Depo Provera appears to be that hormones cause sexual assault and molestation. Currently there are insufficient data to justify this assumption. However, many men with high testosterone levels (1100 or more) neither rape nor molest. In reality, the extent to which biochemical, neurological and genetic factors increase aggression is not yet known.

3)   Sexual assault is defined as a crime of violence.   There is no certainty that the chemical reduction of the libido also reduces aggression (Berlin & Meinecke, 1981).[16]

4)   Use of Depo Provera necessitates costly medical procedures involving comprehensive hormone studies and ongoing testosterone level monitoring.

5)   Reliance on chemically controlling behavior removes individual accountability from the sex offender and does not address the issue of causation.

6)   Because of the various side effects, Depo Provera must be used with extreme caution with individuals with certain physical diseases such as epilepsy, migraines, asthma, and renal and cardiac dysfunction (Bradford, 1983).

7)   When patients stop taking Depo Provera, sexual fantasies and libido return (Bradford, 1983; Gilgun & Gordon, 1985). Hence, the drug must be used indefinitely and be carefully monitored.   Psychotherapy often is combined with the use of Depo Provera, but implementation is not always feasible. Since Depo Provera lowers arousal, behavioral management techniques such as desensitization may prove ineffective while the drug is being used.

8)   Depo Provera affects arousal but not direction.   Pedophiles, who seek emotional intimacy with children and for whom sexual arousal often is of secondary importance, may not benefit from the use of this drug.

---

[16]Berlin and Meinecke, reporting on clinical studies at John Hopkins, assert that Depo Provera has been found to be effective in suppressing sadistic fantasies, and thus, violent, sexual behavior.

9)   While Depo Provera diminishes arousal, it does not affect penile reactions (Langevin, 1983). When using antiandrogens, it is necessary to have a coordinated treatment plan involving a multitude of supportive and educational interventions including provisions for substitute sexual outlets for offenders in therapy.

Cyproterone Acetate (CPA)

CPA is a synthetic steroid similar in structure to progesterone. Use of this antiandrogen to decrease libido was first described in 1967. Like Depo Provera, CPA has a number of problems associated with its use, and a number of side effects including testicular atrophy, fatigue, depression, loss of body hair, and decrease of sebaceous gland secretion (Langevin, 1983). It has no effect on the libido of patients suffering from organic brain disease and exacerbates existing psychoses among the mentally ill (Bradford, 1983).

On August 21, 1985, the Mesa Tribune (Mesa, Arizona), reported the UPI story, "Castrated Man Convicted; Jailed for Child Molestation." A sixty-nine-year-old man had been voluntarily castrated in 1945 after sexually abusing two young girls. A Pasadena Supreme Court Judge offered him the choice of voluntary castration or incarceration. The offender chose to have his testicles surgically removed. Court-ordered castration was legal in 1946, although the practice was halted in the mid 1970's by the Supreme Court as cruel and unusual punishment. Forty years after the offense and subsequent castration, this perpetrator sexually abused two girls, aged eight and five, for which he received a sentence of imprisonment. In practice, castration may be an effective control of deviance only in some cases.

Clearly, candidates for use of experimental antiandrogen therapy must be carefully chosen. Clear guidelines need to be established, and monitoring is essential, since the drug is dose-dependent and the effects are reversible. Bradford (1983) stresses the need for additional studies, especially regarding the correlation between serum testosterone and aggression.

Other authorities concur, stressing the fact that the relationship between biological variables and sexual behavior is complex. Cooperative planning and management among psychiatrists, sex therapists and law enforcement personnel are needed when considering the administration of antiandrogens. Finally, the cost of administration, medical risks, and the experimental nature of the drugs used compound the problems involved in considering widespread implementation.

Community-Based Group Models

Community-based group treatment models for incestuous offenders are becoming so widespread that they merit separate attention in this overview of therapeutic approaches. The prototype for many of these programs operating throughout the country is Parents United. Over ten years ago, Henry Giarretto implemented this treatment program for incestuous families in Santa Clara, California. The program involved the coordination of services from the criminal justice system, probation department, child protective services, police and county attorneys. Incest offenders enter a plea and generally serve short-term jail sentences. They and their families then enter individual and/or marital therapy while simultaneously participating in self-help groups called Parents United and Daughters and Sons United. Although controversial, the program now has many chapters nationwide, and the success rate apparently is quite high (Kroth, 1979).

Other Treatment Methods

Human development courses, i.e., structured educational classes for sex offenders, have proliferated in recent years, both in institutions and in outpatient treatment centers. They constitute an important adjunctive therapy and include courses in stress management, values and attitude clarification, anger control, social skills training, parenting, chemical abuse, human sexuality, and sex-role stereotyping. SAR (Sexual Attitude Reassessment) Seminars, conducted from two to five days, include lectures, small group discussion, and audiovisual materials related to sexual issues and values.

Although group work continues to be the recommended modality with sexually aggressive men, conventional approaches such as psychotherapy are still being used along with a number of innovative methods, such as use of sexual surrogates (prostitutes) and ex-offenders for peer counseling. Other commonly-used approaches include:

1) Treatment by criticism (direct confrontation)

2) Cerebral therapy (bibliotherapy focusing on positive thinking, self-hypnosis, and systematic desensitization)

3) Bioenergetics (for releasing affect)

4) Crisis induction (to assess actual growth potential)

5) Milieu therapy (also called environmental manipulation)

6) Modeling and identification

All of the treatment methods described above have some merits and drawbacks. Selection of programs and therapeutic modalities for given perpetrators, however, must not be indiscriminate but, rather, based on such factors as the type of offense, chronicity, progressive deterioration, level of functioning and others. Initial assessment is the key factor in determining which treatment course, if any, to prescribe. In addition, an individualized treatment plan, focusing on the whole person and not just the symptom, must be formulated for each offender.

Thus far, although differences are recognized among sexually aggressive men, the same treatment approaches have been recommended for them all. Moreover, follow-up and periodic reassessment is essential when working with felons who have committed crimes against persons. A team approach with a combination of interventions is advocated. For example, a chemical-abusing rapist might be seen individually for aversive therapy while concomitantly attending marital therapy, group sessions and Alcoholics Anonymous.   Coordination among probation or parole officers and the various therapists involved ensures adequate monitoring.   Periodic changes in team staffings among professionals relieve burn-out and frustration among workers and provide valuable feedback.   Finally, more research on outcome variables and success rates is essential.

9

THE GROUP EXPERIENCE

For addictive personalities, group therapy affords a number of advantages over individual therapy. The ideal treatment plan, however, involves a program designed to meet the individualized needs of each offender, and may include one-on-one sessions and marital or relationship therapy as well as group therapy.

Advantages of Group Therapy

1) Sex offenders are heavily defended and heavily entrenched in denial, minimization, and rationalization. They tend to resist the directness implicit in one-on-one treatment, particularly since individual therapy affords little opportunity to break through the impasses related to feelings of differentness, alienation and isolation. During pretherapy, the offender, lacking confidence and adhering to a basically pessimistic world-view, invests much energy in rationalizing to preserve his fragile self-esteem. He feels as if he is the only male who has committed shameful and illegal actions. Group confrontation rapidly breaks through the impasse of denial and the group members provide an

atmosphere of tolerance, belonging and acceptance that facilitates deeper disclosures while alleviating guilt and embarrassment.

2) Sex offenders tend to have a limited repertoire of behavioral and emotional responses that provide predictable gratifications. In describing the personalities of compulsive gamblers, Livingston provides some valuable insights into behavioral and emotional patterns among addictive personalities such as sex offenders. He (Livingston, 1974) notes that gamblers deal in absolutes, where every setback is perceived as a catastrophe. In addition, the thought or fantasy of misdeeds is immediately translated into the deed itself, which causes severe anxiety and exacerbates stress to the degree that recidivism becomes likely or even inevitable.

In order to maintain normal functioning and preserve self-image, sex offenders compartmentalize feelings through denial, avoidance and withdrawal. They are emotionally constricted and blocked on an affective level, especially with regard to feelings related to unconscious or conscious aggression.

The group offers a safe, honest and caring atmosphere for eliciting both suppressed and here-and-now feelings through such commonly-known phenomena as contagion, shared cathartic release and confrontation (Maslow, 1967).

A self-governing approach to group therapy enhances self esteem and increases leadership skills. In addition, the group experience affords an opportunity for shared reality-testing and problem-solving. Offenders are given an opportunity to change dysfunctional thinking patterns and reformulate values (Samenov's, 1964).[1] Group therapy also affords an opportunity for participants to practice new roles in a safe setting.

3)   Sex offenders are socially isolated, secretive males with low self-worth, a basic mistrust of others, and a limited world-view. They tend to lack interpersonal commitments on a deep level. Escapism and withdrawal are familiar coping mechanisms which enhance fear, alienation, lack of direction and conflicts related to autonomy and dependence.

Group therapy provides these men with support, validation from others and a sense of commonality of experience. The group becomes a substitute family where each new entrant is like a child confessing and awaiting absolution and direction.

Peele (1976) notes that addiction evolves from a person's subjective response to something that is safe and reassuring. The addict becomes dependent on the source of gratification. His ability to deal with the environment and his "self" is diminished (Peele, 1976). The group helps to enlarge an offender's closed world. Once formerly unsharable secrets are disclosed, the energy focused on pretense, (a socially acceptable image, created to maintain a vulnerable sense of self and self-worth) can be freed.

4)   Sex offenders lack empathy for victims, partly due to unresolved early life trauma, often involving physical and/or sexual abuse, and resulting either in identification with aggressors or displaced anger. These men basically

---

[1]Samenov's phenomenological approach to rehabilitation of criminals involves restructuring and altering errors in their world-view and thought processes.

appear narcissistic, self-centered, opportunistic, and manipulative. They objectify and exploit others to meet their own needs. Through direct victim-confrontation in the here-and-now, regression therapy, bioenergetics and role plays, offenders in group therapy are able to re-experience and repeat childhood trauma in a safe atmosphere which often may result in catharsis, followed by new self-understandings (Alexander and French, 1946).

5) Sex offenders lack social skills such as assertiveness, impulse control, and the knowledge of appropriate vehicles for stress management. Likewise, they lack basic information regarding male-female sex-role stereotyping and human sexuality. Didactic material easily is shared in the group and discussion is stimulated through the sharing of individual experiences and shared reading materials.

6) Sex offenders, like other addictive and dependent personalities such as alcoholics and gamblers, respond to monitoring, support and confrontation as a deterrent to recidivism. Like Alcoholics Anonymous, the group provides a superego transference figure (parent) that exhorts the ego to stand up for itself (Ruitenbeek, 1970). In other words, sex offenders not only have difficulties mediating with reality, they also have impaired superego development. In Freudian terms, the group replaces or augments the superego, offering both support and the monitoring of behaviors.

In the language of Transactional Analysis, sexually aggressive men have an active child (id) and a poorly functioning adult (ego) and parent (superego). The adult is helped in mediation with reality through the operation of an external parent (group). The child is nurtured, but not coddled or allowed to dominate functioning.

7) Sex offenders, with their limited emotional repertoire, tend to sexualize relationships. Some see themselves as predatory seducers, always trying to prove their sexual prowess. The complexities of interpersonal relationships are alien to their world-view which includes the madonna-whore dichotomy, and the double standard in which good women are not allowed to engage in premarital or extra-marital relationships. Their focus is phallic; their primary aim, arousal. Group therapy affords these men with an opportunity to develop empathic and intimate responses to others, both female and male, and to see how their self-centered behavior affects people in their environment.

Thus, the group therapy modality is highly recommended. It provides the elements of catharsis, insight, universality, hope and identification in a safe environment where new behaviors can be modeled. Heppner discusses the value of the group experience for men, in general, whom he feels have dysfunctions related to restrictive emotional control (O'Neil, 1980); interpersonal relations (Aries, 1977; Booth, 1972; Olstad, 1975); homophobia (Fasteau, 1974); sexual performance (Goldberg, 1979); and intimacy (Lewis, 1978). The group experience focuses on communication, inter-personal relating skills and penetration of defenses such as denial (Heppner, 1981).

Goals and Objectives of Group Therapy

The goals of group therapy for sex offenders are: 1) to provide adjunctive, ongoing support in a safe, secure and consistent setting; 2) to monitor abusive behaviors in conjunction with primary therapists, adult probation, parole personnel, and child protective services special-ists, and; 3) to therapeutically intervene into abusive behaviors. The objectives for reaching these goals involve specific therapeutic interventions such as victim-confrontation, role plays and the use of didactic materials, as well as adherence to the norms and values of the group, such as regular participation, nonrecidivist behavior, nonviolence, abstinence from chemical use, and others.

In describing the dynamics of Gamblers Anonymous, Livingston (1974) discusses how recidivism affects group goals. Recognizing that the goal of group therapy is abstinence (or, in the case of sex offenders, nonrecidivist behavior), Livingston notes that the process is rehabilitation. Recidivists are "low" on abstinence, but they do not challenge the actual process of rehabilitation. In fact, in some ways, they reinforce the process by setting examples for other members by reminding all participants how much the group is needed. In addition, group therapy protects its integrity from the threat of recidivism by asserting directly or covertly that recidivists are not sincere group participants.

So powerful are group norms that participants often react more negatively to evasion and lies regarding recidivist behavior than to the actual acting out itself. Like gamblers, sex offenders offer three types of explanations for re-offending: 1) "I don't know why I did it"; 2) "I was under a lot of stress"; and, 3) "I had no choice—my child was there" (Livingston, 1974).[17]

Unlike gamblers, the situation for sex offenders who recidivate is quite serious in terms of legal ramifications. Recidivist behavior, or new disclosures about already-known molestations, must be reported to the authorities. Prospective group members should be advised of this rule prior to their entering group therapy (Beasley and Childers, 1985). Pre-molest behavior, such as encouraging a victim to sit on an offender's lap for possible stimulation, and fantasies

---

[17]One sex offender stated that, in order for him to commit incestuous acts with his daughter, "All the elements had to add up to ten; my daughter had to be there; my job had be to pressured; my wife had to be frigid, etc."

about molestation, need not be reported.[18]   Group members are encouraged to process and deal with these issues within the group.

General Group Format and Procedural Guidelines

Groups for sex offenders differ, depending upon a number of variables, including referral sources, the experience of therapists and funding sources.   For example, therapists receiving state or federal funding for group therapy for chemical abusers will be selective in choosing alcoholic or drug abusing offenders for participation in their programs.

In general, it is recommended that the group be informally arranged with spontaneous topics encouraged from participants. Social censorship should be discouraged and the climate ideally should foster a supportive yet analytic approach to problem-solving and sharing.

The following are some general guidelines related to format and procedures for establishing an ongoing therapy group for sexually aggressive males.

Criteria for Admission

1)   Admission of sex offense.   Generally, it is best to admit men to group therapy who have acknowledged their offenses prior to entering the group. Some offenders, however, do not break through the impasse of denial until the second or third group session.   If denial persists after five or six sessions, it is advisable to discharge the participant.

---

[18]States vary in reporting laws. Arizona, for example, requires that professionals report sexual abuse if they interview victims. Many therapists, however, advise prospective clients that, for ethical reasons, all child sex offenders will be reported even if the victims are not seen.

Offenses should be/have been reported to the appropriate authorities (the police or child protective services or both) by the time the participant enters group therapy. It is best to admit men who have committed similar offenses. The dynamics of rape, incest, exhibitionism and pedophilia vary as do suggested therapeutic interventions. It is possible, however, to allow for some heterogeneity depending upon the personalities of the offenders and their histories. For example, some exhibitionists do have histories of incestuous abuse, and many out-of-home molesters also have sexually abused one or more of their children.

2)   History of nonviolent behavior.   Many sex offenders are potentially violent and have acted out aggressively in the past through wife-battering or physical abuse of their children.   Individual therapists should evaluate the history of violent behavior for each offender, and the potential for future acting out.   Men with convictions for violent acts should be excluded from the group.   In addition, the prognosis is less guarded for those offenders who have an absence of reported aggressive acts in their backgrounds.

3)   Abstinence of chemical abuse for offenders with identified abuse issues.   Participation in Alcoholics Anonymous (AA) or Narcotics Anonymous (NA) should be mandatory for any sexually aggressive male with a history of chemical abuse.

4)   Absence of severe psychopathology. Prospective group members should be evaluated by clinical psychologists before entering group therapy to screen them for severe mental problems such as psychosis.   Psychological testing is not always possible.   However, reports from adult probation, adult parole, and child protective services personnel, as well as from therapists previously seen by an offender, should be reviewed prior to accepting the men into the group.

5) I.Q. (Intelligence Quotient) above the mentally defective range. Participants must have the capacity to assimilate cognitive insights and translate them into behavioral change. In addition, men with limited intellectual capacities require inordinate patience and repetition, and can disrupt the group process through interjection of irrelevant issues.

6) Involvement with a primary therapist, (masters or doctoral level), with experience working with sex offenders. Group therapy is adjunctive to individual treatment and every offender should be seen on a one-to-one basis, either prior to, or concomitant with, group involvement. In addition, while group therapy is largely based on the self-help concept with senior members serving as paraprofessional co-facilitators, at least one doctoral or masters level therapist should be present at all times.

Length of Program

Some therapists organize their groups into phases, i.e., six months of intensive therapy with three-hour groups meeting once or twice per week, followed by six months of weekly group sessions and a one year follow-up on a monthly basis. However, the most successful and dynamic groups are less structured, more open-ended, and variable, with individual treatment plans formulated on the basis of the type of offense, case history and legal mandates for each participant.

As in Alcoholics Anonymous, the underlying philosophy is that sex offenders have life-long control issues. Hence, even after their discharge, group therapy should be available to offenders for feedback and support during periods of change and stress in their lives.

One advantage to the open-ended, long-term group experience is that it affords socially-isolated men an opportunity to form friendships. In addition, senior members implement gains and assume leadership roles which further enhances their self-esteem.   However, in general, steady group attendance on a weekly basis will not exceed two years.

Group Size and Composition

The ideal size for most therapy groups is between eight and twelve participants.   As noted above, groups should be somewhat homogeneous, but some degree of heterogeneity, in terms of the nature of offenses, ages, and socio-economic class strata of the participants, serves to broaden and enrich the group experience for participants.   Because victim confrontation is an integral part of group therapy, having adult female victims present in the group is a valuable therapeutic tool for increasing empathy among offenders. A couples group, or the presence of wives in a group, also enhances perspectives and facilitates communication between the sexes.   It is a useful means to decrease sex-role stereotyping and to work on issues related to male-female sexuality.

The couples or mixed-sex group provides additional advantages for male sex offenders by creating a social microcosm in which to develop new patterns of communication, deal directly with maladaptive behaviors, confront stereotyping, learn new social skills, focus on here-and-now interactions between the sexes, and practice reality testing (Beasley and Childers, 1985).   Particularly with incest couples, working in group therapy helps to break through their unconscious game of collusion and interdependence by confronting the dysfunctional dynamic that binds them together.

Key issues related to the violation of boundaries, mutual self-worth, sexual dysfunction, and adult-child reactions, can be dealt with directly in group sessions.   In addition, couples in therapy groups help wives to develop empathy for their victim-children as the men are confronted to admit the exact nature of their offenses which the women are encouraged to visualize.

There are, however, disadvantages to heterogeneous, mixed-sex groups. Some studies report that homogeneous or same-sex groups tend to promote intimacy and sharing among women but not among men. The ideal group format, thus, might involve alternating same-sex with mixed-sex sessions.[19]

Finally, especially in incestuous families, siblings often are neglected as the focus remains on the triad of victim-spouse-offender. An occasional father-son group is helpful, both to non-victim children and to their fathers who lack parenting skills and, often, have been physically abusive to their children. Hence, variety in format is recommended, depending upon the needs of the particular client population (Gazda, 1971).

Leadership

Paired male and female co-facilitators are recommended so that all members can identify with one of their leaders. Also, the leadership itself provides a model for interpersonal relating between the

---

[19]During one group therapy session in the Phoenix metropolitan area in the Spring of 1985, I invited a group of seven male and female adult victim siblings, ages twenty-five to thirty-five, all of whom had been sadistically sexually abused by their natural father during their first three years of life. Spontaneous regression of one of the siblings had triggered partial memories in other brothers and sisters, all of whom had repressed early trauma and suffered from a variety of symptoms, including splitting, self-mutilation, hypersexual behavior, and psychogenic heart palpitations. The meeting triggered memories for some of the siblings and allowed for ventilation. One of the male victims tried to physically attack an offender who reminded him of his father. Victims and offenders spontaneously restrained this young man who stated that he had never had an opportunity to express his anger, and at the time, "felt like a two-year-old boy who couldn't speak—only react physically to express feelings."

sexes. Here again, however, there are no rigid rules. The presence of a female therapist in an all-male offender group, however, is highly recommended since many of the participants have dysfunctions related to communication with women, sex-role stereotyping, and the lack of knowledge of female sexuality.

An issue rarely dealt with in the literature relates to the therapist as a variable. Professionals tend to avoid critical self-examination and are heavily invested in protecting their privileged status. When conflicts arise between a therapist and a client, the client inevitably is perceived to be the cause, due to personality defects, resistance or transference reactions. The therapist's characteristics (personality, style, sex, age and therapeutic approach) seem immune from critical examination. These factors, however, are relevant variables in successful group facilitation. Inflexible, controlling personalities, for example, detract from the group process with sex offenders. Often, in the backgrounds of sexually aggressive men, lurk excessively authoritarian parents who contributed to the development of undetected deviance and evasion in their offspring. For these men, honesty led to punishment; hence, lying and manipulation were learned behaviors that proved rewarding.

In addition, issues related to the effects of acculturation and socialization merit self-examination among group facilitators. Male therapists should guard against unconscious identification resulting in defensiveness, while female therapists should be aware of the power differential between the sexes, as well as of victim-identification.

Each sex should work to counteract adversarial male-female positions that arise in groups composed of female victims/wives and male offenders.

An effective way for therapists to enhance their own growth is to work with all populations involved in violent and abusive behavior, i.e., victims of every age, spouses and offenders. Until professionals have become experienced in dealing with the spectrum of issues involved in victimization, they will lack perspective and the ability to diffuse rigid positions regarding sex offenses.

A democratic style of leadership is most effective for a client population that needs to develop self-control and autonomous functioning. Therapists should present themselves as distinct from theory and technique, and should be aware of their own reactions, patterns of participation, group tensions and group conflicts.

Group Content and Process

Highly structured, cognitive groups with a preponderance of didactic material and a focus on behavioral management techniques will be short-lived. Sex offenders are a highly volatile population with unresolved emotional difficulties necessitating expressive or affective therapeutic approaches. The expressive or affective format, therefore, is recommended rather than the didactic group approach. Therapists who fall into the parent-instructor roles will elicit indifference, boredom and even resentment among offenders.

Men with low self-images and control problems do not need therapists who, themselves, often have the same difficulties. What they do need are facilitators, shrewd and skilled enough to recognize their own limitations when dealing with a criminal population, and integrated and confident enough to relinquish power without feeling threatened.

The emotional climate of the group experience should be conducive to intense, often cathartic work. This work is facilitated and enhanced by a variety of therapeutic tools, including direct victim-confrontation, psychodrama, hot-seat confrontation, role plays, bioenergetics, regression therapy and bibliotherapy. Participants should be encouraged to write about their backgrounds and offenses to read to the group, to share books and articles relevant to group issues, to help facilitate the group, and to make themselves available, between group sessions, to other offenders in need of support.

The sharing of didactic material is important, but secondary to affective work. Here-and-now sharing, role-playing and practicing assertiveness and communication skills, for example, are stressed over giving lectures or reports on books about these topics.

Group norms are both implicit and explicit, and adherence to the values and standards of the group often is a topic of heated discussion. Chemical use by men with identified abuse issues, for example, is processed in the larger context of responsibility to self and others, and is perceived as a threat to all participants.

The flexibility of the group process diminishes inhibitions and encourages members to problem-solve issues with the realization that the group is available for reality testing. When one offender worries that his nonabused son feels guilty about incestuous abuse perpetrated in the home, he knows that group members not only will provide him with feedback, but may also offer group time for a fathers-sons session to further clarify the issue.

Group members also know that their work includes restitution in the form of helping victims who may or may not be group members. Victims who need an opportunity to confront offenders in person may be brought to group for the sole purpose of allowing them to ventilate. Ventilation by victims provides a needed release for their anger and helps sex offenders experience victim empathy. Outsiders from the community—agency directors, attorneys, and others—may also be invited to the group in the hope of facilitating an understanding of abusive behaviors.

Finally, group participants are given ultimate responsibility for the inclusion or exclusion of members. It is the group which decides whether or not a prospective entrant is so fully entrenched in denial that he is an inappropriate candidate for the group process. So, too, if an offender continues to violate group norms via chemical abuse or pre-molestation behaviors, he may be "voted out" of the meetings.

Thus, the important variables for a successful, long-term group for sex offenders relate to style of leadership, adherence to norms and values, focus on affective work, and flexibility of format. A highly structured group format with an authoritarian leader will prove ineffective with a population of sexually aggressive males.

One method to monitor growth is to be aware of the evolutionary stages through which a successful group passes. Tuckman describes four stages of group growth which culminate in the formation of a group identity:

Forming: A period of exploring purpose and
                  process;

Storming: a period of testing the limits of the
                  group experience;

Norming: a period when group relations and goals
                  are resolved into an identity; and,

Performing: a period when identities of members
                  are merged for task accomplishment.

Bennis and Shepard (1956) describe a two-stage evolutionary process from concern with authority (dependence) to concern with intimacy (interdependence). The important point is that successful groups culminate in the formation of a group identity or collective merging of individual identities that allows for unified task accomplishment.

Coercive Therapy

Many professionals have questioned the efficacy of forced or coercive therapy, i.e., therapy mandated by the criminal justice system. Most sex offenders in treatment are under the jurisdiction of probation and parole departments and have been ordered into individual and/or group therapy. Traditionally, coercive treatment has not been viewed favorably by the therapeutic community.

As opposed to force or coercion, neurotic misery or suffering has been considered the necessary motivator for change via voluntary admission into treatment (Dollard and Miller, 1950). Character-disordered individuals have been perceived as poor candidates for therapy, partly because their personality defects preclude the possibility of guilt and remorse, antecedents to the pain and suffering necessary for positive therapeutic outcomes.

First, the presence of neurotic misery does not automatically signify a desire to change behavioral or emotional patterns. Therapists can attest to the presence, in their client populations, of a number of individuals who are heavily invested in their pain and are desirous merely of long-term therapeutic support along with an opportunity to ventilate.

Second, if viewed on a continuum, antisocial behavior is seen in different degrees and manifestations. On one end of the continuum are the criminal psychopaths, while at the other end are the less seriously impaired individuals with the capacity to experience narcissistic suffering. This can be a powerful motivator when the alternative to change is incarceration.

Confidentiality

The issue of confidentiality merits special attention since group members are criminal felons. Confidentiality can and should be maintained for issues not related to current or past molestation or sexual assault. As noted earlier, current abuse should be reported both for therapeutic and ethical reasons, if not legal ones. Sex offenders habitually manipulate and project responsibility for their behaviors. Therapy will be ineffective in the absence of ownership of offending behaviors.

Individual therapists differ regarding the need to report past sexual offenses to the authorities, offenses that legally fall within the statute of limitations and/or might be considered, "prior bad acts," in court proceedings. Therapists treating criminals find themselves in a dilemma exacerbated by the conflict between moral and ethical questions, and therapeutic concerns.   There are no easy answers to the reporting dilemma.   When considering "prior bad acts," it is best to individualize each situation and to consult other professionals for feedback.

For those therapists whose communications legally are considered privileged (usually certified clinical psychologists and psychiatrists) the issue seems to be resolved.   Nonetheless, in Arizona, during 1985, a Superior Court judge ordered a psychiatrist to repeat privileged communication to the court, communication involving a confession of sexual molestation and murder of a young child.   The rationale for the order rested on the fact that the disclosure by the defendant to the psychiatrist occurred in a hallway after the therapeutic hour had ended.   The psychiatrist's testimony resulted in a guilty verdict against the defendant.

Involuntary Discharge

Offenders who do not adhere to group norms and rules may be involuntarily terminated from group.   Among the reasons for discharging an uncooperative participant are:

1) Persistent denial or minimization regarding sex offenses

2) Three unexcused absences from group

3) Uncooperative behaviors or attitudes

4) Re-offending behaviors

5) Continued chemical abuse

Disadvantages of Group Therapy

Although the recommended therapeutic modality for work with sex offenders, group therapy still poses certain disadvantages or pitfalls. First, group becomes the reference group for members and often replaces the family. The characteristics of this substitute family can begin to resemble the natural family of sexual aggressives by becoming insular, secretive and enmeshed. In effect, the group can become a shelter, protecting participants from painful reality. New behaviors and learnings must transfer from the group to the real world or the process becomes dysfunctional.

Second, the power of the group can have either a positive or a negative effect on its members. The group must be monitored closely by facilitators so that contagion does not result in tyranny.

In one group therapy session, members listened attentively as an incest offender, a long-time participant who sexually abused his teenage daughter, announced that his second daughter, aged eight, disclosed to her school nurse that he had molested both her and her sister. The offender denied the allegation. Group members immediately spoke in his defense. The implicit group norm relating to victim credibility quickly was forgotten as members felt threatened by the allegation and reacted to their own fears of recidivism.

Livingston (1974) discusses the dangers of members who become too protective of the group experience. He notes that one manifestation of protectiveness is seen in the group's reaction to other therapeutic approaches. Members are threatened by therapeutic modalities other than group therapy, and often are quite verbal in their stance against psychiatry, believing that understanding and acceptance can be found only in the group experience. Heppner believes that an additional pitfall relates to the defenses men use to protect their self-images and avoid disclosure, i.e., intellectualization, minimization and denial (1981). Men may try to "hide" in group by withdrawal or by diversionary tactics such as focusing on peripheral issues or assuming leadership roles before they are ready.

To counteract the above pitfalls, the group should be kept open via the introduction of new members from varying backgrounds and by frequent discussion of concepts and issues that stimulate controversy and conflict. Open feedback mechanisms should also be encouraged through the introduction of guest speakers and community members invited to attend sessions. With sensitive facilitators skilled in screening appropriate participants and in monitoring group process, the group experience can be one of the most productive therapeutic modalities for controlling sexually aggressive men.

PART III:

HELPFUL LISTINGS AND FORMS

(A) SYMPTOMS OF RELAPSE FOR GROUP AWARENESS AND DISCUSSION

CHANGES IN FEELINGS AND ATTITUDES

Adamant commitment that it cannot happen again

(Increased) fantasizing and wishful thinking (obsessive)

Egocentric and self-centered thinking

Depression, apathy, and hopelessness

Feelings of failure or actual failure or loss

Self-pity

Lying and manipulation

Defensiveness

Tunnel vision

Feeling stress build-up or overload

Anger and irritability

General dissatisfaction

Denial, minimization, and rationalization

Anxiety, apprehension, tension, and confusion

Immature wish to be happy

Boredom

PHYSICAL COMPLAINTS, CHANGES, AND PROBLEMS

Sleep problems

Psychosomatic problems (gastric distress, headaches, backaches, etc.)

Onset of illness

Sexual changes or indifference

Change in appetite

BEHAVIORAL CHANGES

Life changes (such as job loss) compounding stress

Impulsive behavior

Compulsive behavior

(Resumed/increased) chemical abuse

Social isolation

Indifference or avoidance about getting help

Changes in sex life and/or sexual functioning

Loss of commitments and/or daily discipline

(B) THERAPEUTIC ISSUES
FOR GROUP DISCUSSION

SEXUALITY

Intimacy
Nonsexual expressions of affection
Sex-role stereotyping
Male-female sexual needs

SELF-DESTRUCTIVE THOUGHTS AND BEHAVIORS

Fantasizing
Obsessive thoughts/compulsive behaviors
Chemical abuse
Suicide and suicidal equivalents
Addictive behaviors (work, gambling, etc.)

SOCIAL ISOLATION

Alienation
Avoidance and withdrawal

RESPONSIBILITY

Defensive reactions (denial, minimization,
     rationalization, projection, displacement)
Ownership of behaviors, thoughts, feelings

EXPLOITATIVE BEHAVIORS (WORLD VIEW)

Objectification of others (lack of empathy)
Manipulation, lying, "conning"

PARENTING AND FAMILY NEEDS

Communication (attending behaviors, assertiveness,
   "I" messages, honesty)
Maturity
Family roles and role reversals

FAMILY AND SEXUAL HISTORY

Unmet needs for nurturance
Childhood trauma (physical, emotional, and sexual abuse)

AFFECTIVE RESPONSES

Anger (sublimation, compensation, passive-aggressiveness,
   suppression, repression)
Guilt, remorse (absence of), shame
Impulsivity (lack of control)

STRESS MANAGEMENT

Relaxation skills
Behavioral management of stress
Awareness of triggering events

PROBLEM SOLVING SKILLS DEVELOPMENT

Conflict management
Environmental manipulation
Communication

SELF-ESTEEM

Peer support (affirmations)
Assertiveness training

(C) GENERAL GROUP GUIDELINES

1) The purpose of group therapy is to foster growth and self-awareness so that each member will learn more appropriate ways to cope with his life. Preventing remolestation is the main goal.

2) Group therapy members should expect confrontation, and sometimes painful work, on past experiences that may have led to molestation, and that continue to affect each participant today. Expect support, also. Group therapy is here to give everyone an opportunity to share feelings and thoughts with others who have experienced the same problem.

3) Here-and-now issues related to communication, chemical abuse, loneliness, sexuality, anger, and control are a major focus of the group. In other words, the group deals with both feelings and behaviors in the past and present.

4) Many group members have problems recognizing and dealing with their anger. The group is a place to learn to express anger verbally and through structured exercises.

5) Group therapy is also a place to learn and to practice an assertive style of communication through a three-step process of: (1) describing situations that concern you; (2) expressing honest feelings about those situations; and (3) requesting a change, whether it be related to the group or to your personal life. People in group therapy learn to feel better about themselves by communicating their needs, wants, and feelings.

6) For some of you, group attendance is mandatory; for others, it is voluntary. In either case, you will be asked to leave the group if you refuse to deal with your issues, if you continue to abuse drugs or alcohol, or if you miss three group sessions without telephoning to explain your absence. Probation and parole officers are notified of any unexplained absences.

7) Confidentiality is respected at all times, except regarding remolestation. Please expect that, if sexual abuse recurs, it will be reported to the authorities. If you are fantasizing about molesting, you should share those feelings in the group. Feelings are not criminal offenses—behaviors are. The group is here to help you deal with fantasies and feelings so that you do not act out in ways that are harmful to others.

8) The group is open-ended; in other words, members join the group as the need arises. In addition, following your discharge, the group is here for periodic support and follow-up. Take responsibility by letting the group facilitators know how you feel you are progressing. You should expect to be in group therapy for at least one year. After about six months, you should expect to be assuming a group leadership and modeling role for new members.

9) In general, group leadership is shared. You are expected to take an active role in helping to create a meaningful group experience for everyone. Usually, decisions are made by group consensus.

10) Those members with drug and alcohol problems are expected to refrain from use, and to attend a program such as AA (Alcoholics Anonymous) that is designed specifically to address chemical abuse.

11) The emotional tone of the group is accepting and non-judgmental. The group is a safe place where you can be yourself, deal with issues, relieve stress, and receive both support and advice. Group members are encouraged to share telephone numbers and contact one another between meetings. Also, members are asked to read recommended books and handouts, and to share insights and learnings with others in the group.

12) Start group therapy by re-owning your power. Avoid phrases such as: "I can't," "I don't know," or "I'll try." Replace them with: "I won't," "I'll need to explore that," and "I will." Speak for yourself by stating: "I feel," instead of, "You make me feel." Take responsibility by listening attentively to others and by recognizing, owning, and sharing your thoughts and feelings.

Client: _____

Date: _____

Therapist: _____

(D) SELF-EVALUATION OF BEHAVIORS IN GROUP

Instructions: Circle the number that represents your
behavior in group.

		Not at all		Some-times	Often		Score
1)	Expresses ideas freely and openly (self-discloses)	1	2	3	4	5	_____
2)	Listens attentively to others	1	2	3	4	5	_____
3)	Gives suggestions/ opinions	1	2	3	4	5	_____
4)	Asks for suggestions and opinions from others	1	2	3	4	5	_____
5)	Accepts feedback well	1	2	3	4	5	_____
6)	Focuses on major issues (past and present)	1	2	3	4	5	_____
7)	Demonstrates (by verbal input and participation) a desire to change	1	2	3	4	5	_____
8)	Confronts others when necessary	1	2	3	4	5	_____

9)   Acts as a team
     member (neither
     dominating nor
     withdrawing)   1   2   3   4   5 _____

10) Helps others disclose
     (i.e., encourages,
     "sponsors")   1   2   3   4   5 _____

11) Adheres to group
     norms and helps set
     standards   1   2   3   4   5 _____

                           Total: _____

Comments:

Please feel free to share your results with others during the feedback
sessions.

Name:_____ Date: _____

(E) SELF-EVALUATION BY GROUP FACILITATOR

	Yes	Some-what	No	Needs Improve-ment
1) Initiates action/ movement	___	___	___	___
2) Shows awareness of evolutionary stages of group	___	___	___	___
3) Monitors direction and tempo	___	___	___	___
4) Fosters decisions by consensus and shared leadership among participants	___	___	___	___
5) Uses humor appropriately	___	___	___	___
6) Promotes relaxed yet productive atmosphere	___	___	___	___
7) Helps with task focus	___	___	___	___
8) Creates nonjudgmen-tal, nonthreatening climate	___	___	___	___

9) Perceives and ex-
    presses both pro-
    cess and content   ___   ___   ___   ___

10) Penetrates emotional
    barriers of members   ___   ___   ___   ___

11) Helps with adherence
    to norms   ___   ___   ___   ___

12) Uses techniques (role
    plays, psychodrama,
    bibliotherapy, etc.)
    as needed   ___   ___   ___   ___

(F) FACILITATOR'S EVALUATION
OF GROUP

	Yes	Some-what	No	Needs Improve-ment
1) Members understand group goals	___	___	___	___
2) Members understand objectives toward meeting group goals	___	___	___	___
3) Emotional tone fosters safety, trust, and self-disclosure	___	___	___	___
4) Group norms are respected	___	___	___	___
5) Resources (books, lectures, etc.) are integrated into sessions	___	___	___	___
6) Target issues (anger, control, sex, etc.) are group focus	___	___	___	___
7) Members feel sense of belonging	___	___	___	___
8) Decisions are made by consensus in adherence with group norms	___	___	___	___

9) Group is cohesive enough
to accept disagreements
and assimilate new
members/ideas   ___   ___   ___   ___

10) Members are demonstrating
measurable behavioral change   ___   ___   ___   ___

11) Leadership functions are
shared   ___   ___   ___   ___

12) Communication is effective,
i.e., use of "I" messages,
attending behaviors, etc.   ___   ___   ___   ___

13) Contagion is productive   ___   ___   ___   ___

14) Humor is appropriate   ___   ___   ___   ___

15) Problem-solving is accom-
plished via generation of
alternatives and feedback   ___   ___   ___   ___

Date: _____

(G) SAMPLE SEXUAL HISTORY FORM

Name: _____ Birthdate: _____

Date: _____ Birthplace: _____

1) Describe your parents:

2) Parents' Occupations?

3) Do you have brothers or sisters? Stepbrothers or step-sisters? Are you the oldest? Youngest?

4) Were/are you closer to one sibling than another? To one parent than another?

5) What/how important was your religious background?

6) Was sex discussed at home? With siblings? With friends? Describe:

7) What were your parents' attitudes about sex? About nudity?

8) Were your parents affectionate with you? With each other? Discuss:

9) How would you describe your parents' marriage?

10)   Did you lie or steal as a child? Wet the bed? Set fires?
      Were you cruel to animals or other children?

11)   How well did you do in school? Did you have friends?
      Social outlets?

12)   Did you have frequent illnesses as a child?   Stomach
      aches? Headaches? Unusual fears or nightmares?

13)   How and from whom did you first learn about sex?

14)   What sex games did you play as a child?   How did you
      feel about these games?

15)   Did you masturbate as a child?   Starting at what age?
      How often? How did you feel about masturbation?

16)   Did any upsetting sexual experiences happen to you as a
      child? To your siblings? To your friends? If so, did you
      tell anyone? What was the reaction?

17)   (Women): How did you first learn about menstruation?
      When did you begin to menstruate? How did you feel?

18)   When did you begin to develop physically? What was your
      reaction?

19)   When did you start to date?   Describe your feelings
      about dating?

20) Describe your first dates, including any sexual touching:

21) Discuss sexual and emotional relationships in your teen years. Describe your first experience with sexual intercourse. Were you orgasmic? How did you feel about this experience?

22) Have you ever had VD? Pain during sex? (Women): Inability to allow penetration? (Men): Inability to achieve/sustain an erection? Inability to ejaculate? Describe:

23) How do you feel about being touched in a nonsexual way? In a sexual way?

24) Did you (do you) use contraceptives? Which kind?

25) Do you read/see pornography? Been to striptease shows? How often?

26) Have you dressed in clothing of the opposite sex? How often? When?

27) Have you ever exposed your genitals in what you consider to be an inappropriate context? Describe:

28) Do you often feel angry or sad before or after sex? If so, describe. If not, how do you feel?

29) Describe your most common sexual fantasy:

30) Have you had homosexual experiences? When? Describe your feelings about these experiences.

31) Describe the kind of emotional commitment you want/need with a partner. Have you experienced this commitment? Often?

32) Have you ever felt dirty or guilty about sex? About your sexual fantasies?

33) Describe yourself as a sexual person:

34) Describe yourself as a man or woman:

35) How important is sex to you? In your relationship?

36) How important is foreplay to you?

37) What aspects about your sexual relationship(s) would you change? How?

38) Have you experienced sexual relationships outside of marriage? How often and how did you feel about it?

39) Have you been able to discuss sex with your partner(s)? Your likes or dislikes?

40) How many times have you been married? Divorced? Discuss.

Write down your first reaction to each of the following:

Menstruation:

Penis:

Vagina:

Vaginal secretions:

Semen:

Oral sex:

Anal sex:

Sex with children:

Forced intercourse:

Sex games:

Intercourse:

Foreplay:

Masturbation:

Sex fantasies:

Manual orgasms:

Rape:

"Peeping":

Different sexual positions:

Sex with animals:

Promiscuity:

Adultery:

Public exposure (exhibitionism):

Obscene telephone calls:

(H) VALUES QUESTIONNAIRE 1

[This questionnaire elicits information regarding impulse/anger control, sexuality, problem-solving skills, moral development, use of defenses, stress management, and social isolation.]

Respond to the following questions in two or three brief sentences:

1) How often do you feel that your boss has been unfair to you? What do you usually do about this?

2) How do you like to spend time, alone or with others? What are your favorite pastimes or hobbies?

3) Which concept makes more sense to you: "An eye for an eye," or "Turn the other cheek?" Explain.

4) How do you feel about women? React to the notion that women fall into two categories—madonnas or whores:

5) Many people say you should spend your money now because, "You can't take it with you." Do you agree?

6) Describe five ways that you usually manage the stresses in your life?

7) If you were in a "jam," whom would you turn to and why?

8) List three aspects of your life that you value and describe the reasons why?

9) Therapists say that depression is defined as anger turned against yourself. Do you agree?

10) React to the statement, "Most people are cons."

11) Do you care what other people think of you? Explain.

12)   React to the statement, "Everyone is capable of murder under the right circumstances":

13)   How honest do you feel you are with people who are important to you?

14)   React to the statement, "It's okay for men to hug each other in affection":

15)   React to the statement, "In the United States, all men are penis-centered":

16)   How do you usually handle your anger?

17)   React to the statement, "Guilt is a useless emotion."

18)   In what one way would you change your life if you could?

(I) VALUES QUESTIONNAIRE 2

[This questionnaire focuses on moral values and concepts of social deviance.]

React to each of the following situations using these guidelines: (A) Is the given situation right or wrong? Harmful to anyone? Meriting legal involvement?   (B) If a friend described these situations to you, implying that he or his child were involved, what advice would you give to him?

1)   Two 12 year old boys engage in mutual masturbation a couple of times.

2)   A 13 year old boy fondles his six year old sister's genitals once.

3)   A man habitually masturbates in his car while watching attractive women on the street.

4)   In the army, without female companionship, two heterosexual men engage in frequent homosexual activities.

5)   A 10 year old boy and his 8 year old sister engage in long term fondling and mutual masturbation.

6)   On a date, a man coerces a woman to have sexual intercourse. She is unwilling and protests, but is not physically hurt in any way.

7)   A teenage boy makes obscene phone calls periodically.

8)   A man peeps in windows, masturbating as he watches females undress or have sex. He is never seen nor caught.

APPENDICES

APPENDIX A:

REFERENCES FOR

PART I: UNDERSTANDING AND ASSESSING SEX OFFENDERS

American Psychiatric Association. *Diagnostic and Statistical Manual of Mental Disorders (DSM-III)*. Washington, DC: APA, 1968, 44; 1980, 272; 3rd Edition, 1980 268-69.

Andrews, L.B. "Mind Control in the Courtroom." *Psychology Today*, March 1982, 14(3).

Bach, G.R., and Goldberg, H. *Creative Aggression*. New York: Avon, 1975, 32 and 87.

Baron, R.A. *Human Aggression*. New York: Plenum, 1977, 223.

Blanchard, W.H. "The Group Process in Gang Rape." *Journal of Social Psychology*, 1959, 49, 259-66.

Borowski, Dr. Jan, Pediatrician, Maricopa Medical Center, Phoenix, Arizona, June 1, 1985, during panel-slide presentation, Echo Mountain School, Phoenix.

Brecher, E.M. *Treatment Programs For Sex Offenders*. Washington, DC: U.S. Dept. of Justice, January 1978, 6.

Brownmiller, S. *Against Our Will.* New York: Simon and Schuster, 1975.

Bulkley, J. (Ed.) *Innovations in the Prosecution of Child Sexual Abuse Cases,* Washington, DC: American Bar Association, National Legal Resource Center for Child Advocacy and Protection, November 1981.

Burgess, A.W., and Holmstrom, L.L. "Rape Trauma Syndrome." *American Journal of Psychiatry,* 1976, 131, 981-6.

Bustanoby, A., *The Ready Made Family: How To Be A Stepparent and Survive.* Grand Rapids, MI: Zondervan Publishing House, 1978, 93.

Callaway, Sylvia, former Director of the Austin, Texas Rape Crisis Center, as reported in Ms, supra, 58.

Cohen, M., Groth, A.N., and Siegal, R. "Clinical Prediction of Sexual Dangerousness," unpublished paper, Center for Diagnosis and Treatment of Sexually Dangerous Offenders, Bridgewater, MA, August 20, 1975.

Comfort, A. (Ed.) *The Joy of Sex: A Cordon Bleu Guide to Lovemaking.* New York: Crown, 1972.

Ellis, A. *The Folklore of Sex.* New York: Charles Boni, 1951, 273.

Fishback, W.P. *A Manual of Elementary Law.* Indianapolis, IN: Bowen-Merril Co., 1896, 400.

Foster, J.D. *Suffer The Little Children.* Portsmouth, OH: Keystone Copy Cat Printing, 1981, 18.

Freedman, L.Z. "Truth Drugs." *Contemporary Psychology: Readings From Scientific American.* San Francisco: W.H. Freeman & Co., 1971, 319-24.

Freund, K. 1982. Cited in Langevin, R., supra, 322-332.

Geiser, R.L., *Hidden Victims: The Sexual Abuse of Children.* Boston: Beacon Press, 1979, 46.

Glaser, D. "Prediction Tables as Accounting Devices for Judges and Parole Boards": *Crime and Delinquency,* July 1962, 8, 239-58.

Glaser, D. Strategic Criminal Justice Planning. Rockville, MD: U.S. Dept. of Health, Education and Welfare, National Institute of Mental Health, 1976, 162.

Goodman, G., & Michelli, J.A. "Would You Believe A Child Witness?" *Psychology Today,* November 1981, 15(11), 83-95.

Goodman, G.S. (Ed.) "The Child Witness." *Journal of Social Issues,* Summer 1984, 40(2).

Goodwin, J., Sahd, D., and Rada, R. "Incest Hoax: False Accusations, False Denials." In: Holder, W.M. (Ed.) *Sexual Abuse of Children: Implications for Treatment.* Englewood, CO: American Humane Association, Child Protection Division, 1980, 37-38.

Gottfredson, D.M. "Assessment Methods." In: Radzinowicz, L., and Wolfgang, M.E. (Eds.) *Crime and Justice, 3, The Criminal Under Restraint.* New York: Basic Books, 1977, 97-100.

Greenback, R.K. "Are Medical Students Learning Psychiatry?" *Pennsylvania Medical Journal,* 1961, 64(8), 989-92.

Groth, N.A. *Men Who Rape: The Psychology of the Offender.* New York: Plenum Press, 1979, 13.

Groth, N.A., and Burgess, A.W. "Rape: A Sexual Deviation," Paper presented at the American Psychological Association Annual Meeting, September 5, 1976, Washington, DC, 8.

Groth, N.A., Hobson, W.F., and Gary, T.S. "The Child Molester: Clinical Observations." In: *Social Work and Child Sexual Abuse.* New York: Haworth Press, Inc., 1982, 134-36.

Hess, E.H. "Attitudes and Pupil Size." *Contemporary Psychology: Readings From Scientific American.* San Francisco: W.H. Freeman & Co., 1971, 400-08.

Holder, W.M.(Ed.), *Sexual Abuse of Children: Implications for Treatment.* Englewood, CO: American Humane Association, Child Protection Division, 1980, 37-38.

Institute of Noetic Sciences, Investigations, 1(3 and 4). Sausalito, CA: Institute of Noetic Sciences, 1985.

Johns, D. "Institutional Program Patterns, Parole Prognosis and Outcome." Research Report #52. Sacramento, CA: Dept. of Youth Authority, 1967.

Jones, E.M. "Abuse Abuse: The Therapeutic State Terrorizes Parents in Jordan, Minnesota." *Fidelity,* February 1985, 4(3), 20-22.

Joyce, C. "Lie Detector." *Psychology Today,* February 1984, 18(2), 6-8.

Kinsey, A., Pomeroy, W.B., Martin, C.E., and Gebbard, P.H. *Sexual Behavior in the Human Female.* Philadelphia: W.B. Saunders, 1953, 705.

Langevin, R. *Sexual Strands: Understanding and Treating Sexual Anomalies in Men.* Hillsdale, NJ: Lawrence Erlbaum Publisher, 1983, 322, 323.

Lester, D. *Unusual Sexual Behavior: The Standard Deviations.* Springfield, IL: Charles C. Thomas, Publisher, 1975, 7-16, 20, 23, 24, 35, 141, 144, 154, 155, 159-64, 209.

MacFarlane, Kee. "The Young Witnesses in the McMartin Sexual Abuse Case Undergo A Legal Battering In Court." *People,* July 8, 1985, 24(2), 26.

Madow, L. *Anger: How to Recognize and Cope With It.* New York: Charles Scribner's Sons, 1972, 53-54.

Maris. R.W. "Deviance as Therapy: The Paradox of the Self-Destructive Female." *Journal of Health/Social Behavior,* 1971, 12(2), 113.

Mayer, A. *Incest: A Treatment Manual for Therapy with Victims, Spouses, and Offenders.* Holmes Beach, FL: Learning Publications, Inc., 1983.

Mayer, A. *Sexual Abuse: Causes, Consequences, and Treatment of Incestuous and Pedophilic Acts.* Holmes Beach, FL: Learning Publications, Inc., 1985, 4, 11, 12, 21.

Meyer, A. "Do Lie Detectors Lie?" In: Sullivan, JJ., Victor, J.L., and MacNamara, D.E.J. (Eds.) *Annual Editions: Criminal Justice 83/84.* Guilford, CT: Duskin Publishing Group, Inc., Sluice Books, 158-59.

Miller, A. *For Your Own Good: Hidden Cruelty in Child Rearing and the Roots of Violence.* New York: Farrar, Straus & Giroux, 1983.

Money, J., and Tucker, P. *Sexual Signatures: On Being a Man or a Woman.* Boston: Little Brown & Co., 1975, 19.

NBC Television, "The Silent Shame," August 1984.

Newsweek, "Rape and the Law." May 20, 1985, 61-64.

Palm, R., and Abrahamsen, D. "A Rorschach Study of the Wives of Sex Offenders." *Journal of Nervous and Mental Diseases,* 1954, 119, 167-72.

Panzetta, A.F. "Toward a Scientific Psychiatric Nosology: Conceptual and Pragmatic Issues." *Archives of General Psychiatry,* 1974, 30(2), 54-61.

Parents United, Brochure, 1985.

People, "The Brave Testimony of a Ten-Year-Old Girl Convicts her Former Foster-Father." July 8, 1985, 24(2), 28-29.

Prescott, J. "Alienation and Affection." *Psychology Today,* December 1979, 124.

Psychology Today, October 1984, 18(10), 80.

Psychology Today, "Lifestyles, Looks Sway Rape Juries, Study Says." October 1985.

Rickels, N.K. "Exhibitionism" *Journal of Social Therapy,* 1955, 1, 168-81.

Rogers, C.M., and Thomas, J.N. "Sexual Victimization of Children in the U.S.A.: Patterns and Trends." Clinical Proceedings. Washington, DC: Children's Hospital National Medical Center, May/June and July/August 1984, 40 (3 and 4) 215-17.

Roxxman, P. *Sexual Experience Between Men and Boys.* New York: Association Press, 1976.

Rubin, S. *Psychiatry and the Criminal Law.* Dobbs Ferry, NY: Oceana, 1965, 93.

Sawyer, J. "Measurement and Prediction, Clinical and Statistical." Psychological Bulletin, September 1966, 178-200.

Schmideberg, M. "On Treating Exhibitionism: Some Implications." *International Journal of Offender Therapy and Comparative Criminology,* 1972, 16(2), 130-137.

Socarides, C.W. "The Development of Fetishistic Perversion." *Journal of the American Psychoanalytic Association,* 1960, 8, 281-311.

Smith, supra, cited in Medical Tribune, Wednesday, June 27, 1984.

Smith, A.B., and Berlin, L. *Treating the Criminal Offender.* Englewood Cliffs, NJ: Prentice-Hall, Inc., 2nd ed., 1981.

Smith, B.M. "The Polygraph." In: *Contemporary Psychology: Readings from the Scientific American.* San Francisco, CA: W.H. Freeman & Co., 1971, 325-31.

Smithyman, S.D. "Characteristics of Undetected Rapists." In: Parsonage, W.H. (Ed.) *Perspectives on Victimology,* Vol. 2. Beverly Hills, CA: Sage Publishers, 1979, 99-119.

Stoller, R. J. *Perversions: The Erotic Form of Hatred.* New York: Pantheon Books, 1975, xiii-xiv, 59.

Sweet, E. "Date Rape: An Epidemic and Those Who Deny It." Ms, October 1985, 14(4), 57, 59.

Szasz, T.S. *Psychiatric Justice.* New York: Macmillan, 1965.

Talent, N. "Sexual Deviation As A Diagnostic Entity: A Confused and Sinister Concept." In: Smith, S. (Ed.), Bulletin of the Menninger Clinic, January 1977, 41(1), 52.

Task Force Report of the American Psychological Association, as reported in the Arizona Republic, "Legal System Traumatizes Victims of Violent Crime, Study Says," December 1, 1984.

Veraa, A. "Probation Officer Treatment for Exhibitionists. Federal Probation, March 1976, 54-55.

Weldy and Associates, Phoenix, Arizona, August 26, 1985.

Whitfield, D. "Tyranny Masquerades as Charity: Who are the Real Abusers?" *Fidelity,* February 1985, 4(3), 14-15.

Woods, S.M., and Matterson, J. "Sexual Attitudes of Medical Students: Some Implications for Medical Education." *American Journal of Psychiatry,* 1967, 124(3), 323-32.

Yalom, I.D. "Aggression and Forbiddenness in Voyeurism." *Archives of General Psychiatry,* 1960, 3, 305-19.

APPENDIX B:

REFERENCES FOR

PART II: MANAGEMENT AND TREATMENT APPROACHES

Alexander and French characterize the re-experiencing of trauma as the key to every "penetrating therapeutic result." Refer to: Alexander, F., and French, T.M. *Psychoanalytic Therapy.* New York: Ronald Press, 1946.

Baily, T.F., and Baily, W.H. *Criminal or Social Intervention in Child Sexual Abuse: A Review and a Viewpoint.* Denver, CO: American Humane Association, 1983, 16-19.

Beasley L., and Childers, J.H. Jr. "Group Counseling for Heterosexual, Interpersonal Skills: Mixed- or Same-Sex Group Composition." *Journal for Specialists in Group Work,* November, 1985, 10(4), 1982-97.

Bennis, W.G., and Shepard, H.A. "A Theory of Group Development." *Human Relations,* 1956, 9, 415-36.

Berlin, F.S., and Meinecke, C.F. "Treatment of Sex Offenders with Anitandrogen Medication: Conceptualization, Review of Treatment Modalities, and Preliminary Findings." *American Journal of Psychiatry,* 1981, 138, 601-07.

Berlin, F.S., and Meinecke, C.F., reporting on clinical studies at Johns Hopkins, assert that Depo Provera has been found to be effective in suppressing sadistic fantasies, and thus violent, sexual behavior. Refer to: Berlin, F.S., and   Meinecke, C.F.   "Treatment of Sex Offenders with Antiandrogen Medication: Conceptualization, Review of Treatment Modalities, and Preliminary Findings." American Journal of Psychiatry, 1981, 138, 601-07.

Bradford, J. McD.   "The Hormonal Treatment of Sex Offenders." Bulletin of AAPL, 1983, 11(2), 163, 164-67.

Brecher, E.M.   *Treatment Programs for Sex Offenders.*   Washington, DC: U.S. Dept. of Justice, National Institute of Law Enforcement and Criminal Justice, January 1978, 9, 10, 85.

Conrad, P.   "On the Medicalization of Deviance and Social Control." In Ingleby, D. (Ed.), *Critical Psychiatry: The Politics of Mental Health.*   New York: Pantheon Books, 1980, 86.

Dollard, J., and Miller, N.E.   *Personality and Psychotherapy.*   New York: McGraw-Hill Book Co., Inc., 1950.

Gazda, G.M.   *Group Counseling: A Developmental Approach.*   Boston: Allyn & Bacon, 1971, 34-36.

Gilgun, F.J., and Gordon, S.   "Sex Education and the Prevention of Child Sexual Abuse."   *Journal of Sex Education and Therapy,* Spring-Summer 1985, 2(1), 50.

Glaser, D.   *Strategic Criminal Justice Planning.*   Rockville, MD: U.S. Dept. of Health, Education, and Welfare, National Institute for Mental Health, 1976, 161, 207.

Hackett, T.P.   "The Psychotherapy of Exhibitionists in a Court Clinic Setting."   Seminar: Psychiatry, 1971, 3(3), 297-306.

Heppner, P.P.   "Counseling Men in Groups."   *Personnel and Guidance Journal,* December 1981, 60(4).

Ingleby, D. (Ed.) *Critical Psychiatry: The Politics of Mental Health.* New York: Pantheon, 1980, 7.

Knopp, F.H. *Retraining Adult Sex Offenders: Methods and Models.* Syracuse, NY: Safer Society Press, 1984, 16.

Kovel, J. "The American Mental Health Industry." In Ingleby, D. (ed.), *Critical Psychiatry: The Politics of Mental Health.* New York: Pantheon Books, 1980, 86.

Kroth, J.S. *Child Sexual Abuse.* Springfield, IL: Charles C. Thomas, Publisher, 1979. This book critiques/evaluates Giaretto's program.

Langevin, R. *Sexual Strands: Understanding and Treating Sexual Anomalies in Men.* Hillsdale, NJ: Lawrence Erlbaum Associates, Publishers, 1983, 50-53, 58, 163, 293.

Livingston, J. *Compulsive Gamblers: Observations on Action and Abstinence.* New York: Harper, 1974, 103-04, 116-118, 126.

MacNamara, D.E.J. "Medical Model in Corrections: Requiescat in Pace." In Montanino, F. (Ed.), *Incarceration: The Sociology of Imprisonment.* Beverly Hills: Sage Publications, 1978.

Maslow refers to the "no crap therapy" of the direct group approach. Refer to: Maslow, A.H. "Synanon and Eupsychia." *Journal of Humanistic Psychology,* Spring 1967.

McNamara, J.R., and Macdonough, T.S. "Some Methodological Considerations in the Design and Implementation of Behavior Therapy Research." *Behavior Therapy,* 1972, 3, 361-78.

Newman, K. "U.K. Licenses Depo Provera." *People,* 1984, 11, 32.

Peele, S. *Love and Addiction.* New York: New American Library/Signet Book, 1976, 6, 56.

Ruitenbeek, H. *The New Group Therapies Book.* New York: Avon: 1970, 168.

Samenov's phenomenological approach to rehabilitation of criminals involves restructuring and altering errors in their world view and thought processes. Refer to: Samenov, S.E. *Inside the Criminal Mind.* New York: Time Books/New York Times Book Co., Inc., 1964, 6.

Sturup, G.K. "The Treatment of Sexual Offenders." Bulletin de la Societe' Internationale de Criminologie, 1960, 320-29.

Sun, M. "Panel Says Depo Provera Not Proved Safe." *Science,* November 23, 1984, 22(4677), 950-51.

Watts, D.L., and Courtois, C.A. "Trends in the Treatment of Men Who Commit Violence Against Women." *Personnel and Guidance Journal,* December 1981, 60(4), 246, 247, 249.

APPENDIX C:

ANNOTATED READING LIST
FOR SEX OFFENDERS
AND THEIR SPOUSES

Adams, C. and Fay, J. *No More Secrets.* San Luis Obispo, California: Impact Publishers, 1981. Deals with sex abuse prevention for parents to use with their children. Increases an understanding of molestation and the effects of victimization.

Armstrong, L. *Kiss Daddy Goodnight: A Speakout on Incest.* New York: Pocket Books, 1978. Portrait of a victim of incestuous abuse. Increases victim empathy.

Bach, G.R. and Goldberg, H. *Creative Aggression: The Art of Assertive Living.* New York: Avon, 1975. Provides numerous examples of the hazards of suppressed anger and elaborates on ways to assertively express feelings.

Berman, S. *The Six Demons of Love: Men's Fears of Intimacy.* New York: McGraw Hill Books, 1984. Deals with men's fears of exposure, vulnerability, loss of self, dependency and anger.

Bloomfield, H.H. *Making Peace with Your Parents.* New York Ballantine Books, 1983. Describes causes of anger, presents sexual scripts and roles; provides suggestions and exercises for reaching resolution with parents.

Brady, K. *Father's Days: A True Story of Incest.* New York: Dell, 1979. Provides personal account of victim of incestuous abuse.

Calhoun, L.G., Selby, J., King, H.E. *Dealing with Crisis: A Guide to Critical Life Problems.* Englewood Cliffs, NJ: Prentice Hall, Inc., 1976. Defines types and causes of life crises including suicide, rape, marital discord and sexual dysfunction; proposes coping mechanisms.

Carnes, P. *Sexual Addiction.* Minneapolis, Minnesota: CampCare Publications, 1983. Describes the addiction cycle, co-addiction, and the twelve-step approach to treatment.

Collins, G.R. *Overcoming Anxiety.* Wheaton, Illinois: Key Publishers, Inc., 1973 Discusses types of anxiety and their origins; offers practical solutions.

Comfort, A. *The Joy of Sex.* New York: Fireside, 1972. Elaborates on ways to enhance sexual enrichment (illustrated).

Conway, J. *Men in Mid-Life Crisis.* Elgin, Illinois: David C Cook Publishing Co., 1983 Provides insights into male life-stage crises.

Davis, M., Eshelman, E., and McKay, M. *The Relaxation and Stress Reduction Workbook.* Richmond, California: New Harbinger Publications, 1981. Gives instructions on relaxation techniques including biofeedback, guided imagery, autogenics, meditation, hypnosis, progressive muscle relaxation and refocused attention.

Dowling, C. *The Cinderella Complex.* New York: Pocket Books, 1982. Focuses on woman's fear of independence with resultant enmeshed relationships.

James, M. *The O.K. Boss.* New York: Bantam, 1976. Introduces reader to T.A. (Transactional Analysis) and the games people in position of authority play.

Kiley, D. *The Peter Pan Syndrome.* New York: Dodd, Mead, 1983. Examines the phenomenon of the adult male who is incapable of acting/behaving maturely.

Kiley, D. *The Wendy Dilemma: When Women Stop Mothering Their Men.* New York: Avon, 1984. Discusses the female role as mother to mate with resultant destructiveness to marital relationships.

Madox, L. *Anger.* New York: Charles Scribner, 1972. Deals with the roots and manifestations of anger.

McCabe, T.R. *Victims No More.* Center City, Minnesota: Hazelton, 1978. Examines alcoholism and co-addiction; describes rational-emotive techniques for change.

Mornell, P. *Passover Men, Wild Women.* New York: Ballantine, 1980. Deals with conflicts in male-female relationships due to personality patterns and communication styles.

Naifeh, S. and Smith, G.W. *Why Can't Men Open Up?* New York: Warner Books, Inc., 1984. Deals with men's problems with intimacy.

Powell, J. *The Secret of Staying in Love.* Niles, Illinois: Argus Communications, 1974. Contains exercises for enhancing intimacy and communication.

Rubin, T.I. *The Angry Book.* New York: Collier Books, 1978. Deals with all aspects of anger and its effects.

Russianoff, P. *Why Do You Think I Am Nothing Without A Man?* New York: Bantam, 1982. Includes insights regarding some women's selfperceptions as being incomplete and lacking, in the absence of validation by men.

Selye, H. *Stress Without Distress.* New York: Lippincott, 1974. Describes the physiological mechanisms of stress and provides specific advice for avoiding its harmful effects.

Smith, G.W. *Couple Therapy.* New York: Collier Books, 1973. Provides forty-seven exercises for developing emotional and physical intimacy.

Stearns, A.K. *Living Through Personal Crisis.* New York: Ballantine, 1984. Examines emotional reactions to loss and gives guidance for crisis management.

APPENDIX D:

OTHER SEXUAL DEVIATIONS

BESTIALITY (also ZOOERASTIA): sexual intercourse between humans and animals.

CABARETING: act of having deviant fantasies and daydreams.

COPROLAGNIA: act of obtaining sexual gratification from eating, smelling, throwing, and handling excrement; related to coprophilia.

COPROPHRASIA: inordinate use of obscene language and pornographic materials.

FLAGELLATION: condition characterized by desire to whip (sadism) or be whipped (masochism) for sexual excitement.

FROTTAGE: act of obtaining sexual satisfaction by rubbing up against another person.

GERONTOPHILIA: use of older persons to obtain sexual gratification.

KLEPTOMANIA: compulsion to steal resulting in sexual excitement.

MASOCHISM: act of obtaining sexual satisfaction through receiving torture, humiliation, pain and suffering.

NECROPHILIA: sexual desire stimulated by corpses.

PARAPHILIA: an anomaly of sexuality.

PIQUERISM: act of obtaining sexual satisfaction from stabbing, piercing, cutting flesh, and shedding blood; related to lust mutilation.

PYGMALIONISM: desire to have sexual contact with inanimate objects such as statues or mannequins.

PYROMANIA: act of obtaining sexual satisfaction from fire-setting.

SADISM: act of inflicting pain on humans and animals, often for sexual gratification.

TRANSVESTISM: compulsion to dress in clothing of the opposite sex.

TIOLISM: form of exhibitionism/voyeurism where participants engage in group sexual activities.

UROLAGNIA (also UROLAGIA): act of associating sexual excitement with urine and urination.

VAMPIRISM: act of sucking blood for sexual excitement.

ZOOPHILIA: unnatural fondness for animals.

ZOOERASTY (also ZOOERASTIA): see BESTIALITY.

INDEX